ADVANCED
COMMON CORE
MATH
EXPLORATIONS

ADVANCED COMMON CORE MATH EXPLORATIONS

Numbers & Operations

JERRY BURKHART

PRUFROCK PRESS INC.
WACO, TEXAS

Prufrock Press Inc.
P.O. Box 8813
Waco, TX 76714-8813
Phone: (800) 998-2208
Fax: (800) 240-0333
http://www.prufrock.com

Table of Contents

A Note to Students

Welcome, math explorers! You are about to embark on an adventure in learning. As you navigate the mathematical terrain in these activities, you will discover that "doing the math" means much more than calculating quickly and accurately. It means using your creativity and insight to question, investigate, describe, analyze, predict, and prove. It means venturing into unfamiliar territory, taking risks, and finding a way forward even when you're not sure which direction to go. And it means discovering things that will expand your mathematical imagination in entirely new directions.

Of course, the job of an explorer involves hard work. There may be times when it will take a real effort on your part to keep pushing forward. You may spend days or more pondering a single question or problem. Sometimes, you might even get completely lost. The process can be demanding—but it can also be very rewarding. There's nothing quite like the experience of making a breakthrough after a long stretch of hard work and seeing a world of new ideas and understandings open up before your eyes!

These explorations are challenging, so you might want to team up with a partner or two on your travels—to discuss plans and strategies and to share the rewards of your hard work. Even if you don't reach your final destination every time, I believe you will find that the journey was worth taking. So gear up for some adventure and hard work . . . and start exploring!

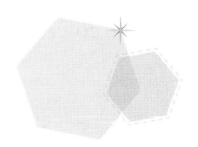

Introduction

This introduction contains general information about the structure of the books and implementation of the activities in the *Advanced Common Core Math Explorations* series. For additional information and support, please see the free e-booklet *Advanced Common Core Math Explorations: A Teacher's Guide* that accompanies this series at http://www.prufrock.com/Assets/ClientPages/AdvancedCCMath.aspx.

AUDIENCE

Advanced Common Core Math Explorations is designed to support students, teachers, and other learners as they work to deepen their understanding of middle school math concepts. The activities have been written primarily with upper elementary and middle school students and teachers in mind. However, older students or those who have already studied more advanced content can also enjoy and benefit from them. The explorations can be used in classrooms, as professional development activities for mathematics teachers, in college math content and methods courses, and by anyone who would like to extend their understanding of middle school mathematics concepts by solving challenging problems.

These explorations are designed to stretch students beyond their initial level of comfort. They are built around the belief that most of us underestimate the mathematics we are capable of learning. Although the activities are challenging, they are also meant to be accessible. Although they are targeted to the special needs of gifted and talented students, I hope that teachers will make them available to any student who would like to pursue the challenge. Most students are capable of making progress and learning something meaningful, even if they work just on the first question or two of an activity.

PURPOSE

The investigations in this series were developed through years of work with talented middle school math students. They are designed to:
- » engage students in the excitement of mathematical discovery;
- » deepen students' understanding of a wide range of middle school math concepts;
- » encourage the use of multiple strategies for solving problems;

» help students become flexible, creative, yet disciplined mathematical thinkers;
» improve mathematical communication skills;
» highlight connections between diverse mathematical concepts;
» develop perseverance, patience, and stamina in solving mathematical problems;
» provide levels of depth and challenge to meet a variety of needs and interests;
» enable students to work both collaboratively and independently; and
» offer opportunities for further exploration.

STRUCTURE OF THE BOOKS

Each book in the *Advanced Common Core Math Explorations* series contains ready-to-use explorations focused on one mathematical content area. The content and structure are built around the Common Core State Standards for Mathematics (National Governors Association Center for Best Practices & Council of Chief State School Officers [NGA & CCSSO], 2010), both the Content Standards and the Standards for Mathematical Practice. Because the emphasis is on challenge and depth, there is a stronger focus on concepts than on procedural skills. However, most activities provide plenty of opportunities to practice computational skills as well.

Each exploration is matched with one or more Common Core benchmarks or clusters, which come with grade-level designations (see p. 8). This grade-level information should serve as a rough guide. When selecting activities, use your own knowledge of your students' backgrounds and abilities. Information about the prior knowledge needed for each exploration is also included as a guide.

FEATURES OF THE EXPLORATIONS

Each activity includes three stages. Stage 1 (and sometimes part of Stage 2) may be challenging enough to meet the needs of many students. The second and third stages are usually appropriate for older students, or for those who finish early, need more challenge, or are highly motivated and curious to learn more. They may also be useful for teachers or other adults who have more mathematical experience and want to extend their own knowledge further. I have separated the explorations into stages in order to provide a tool for setting goals, to help measure and celebrate students' progress, and to create additional options for those who need them.

Each exploration also contains features carefully designed to support teachers in the implementation process: an introduction, the student handout, a set of questions and notes to guide conversation, detailed solutions, and suggestions for a closing discussion.

IMPLEMENTING THE EXPLORATIONS

Implementing each exploration involves five steps on the part of the teacher: prepare, introduce, follow up, summarize, and assess.

Prepare

The best way to prepare to teach an activity is to try it yourself. Although this involves an initial time investment on your part, it pays great dividends later. Doing the activity, ideally with a partner or two, will help you become familiar with the mathematics, anticipate potential trouble spots for students, and plan ways to prepare students for success. After you have used the activity once or twice with students, very little preparation will be needed.

Introduce

The Introduction section at the beginning of each exploration provides support to help you get your students started: materials and prior knowledge needed, learning goals, motivational background, and suggestions for launching the activity.

Read the Motivation and Purpose selection to students, and then follow the suggestions for leading a discussion to help them understand the problem. Often, one of the suggestions involves looking through the entire activity with them (or as much of it as they will be doing) to help them see the big picture before they begin. Let students know what kind of a time frame you have in mind for the exploration. An activity may take anywhere from a few days to 2 or 3 weeks depending on how challenging it is for students, how much of it they will complete, and how much class time will be devoted to it.

The explorations are designed to allow students to spend much of their time working without direct assistance. However, it's usually best if you stay with them for a few minutes just after introducing an activity to ensure that they get started successfully. This way, you can catch potential trouble spots early and prevent unnecessary discouragement.

This is also a good time to remind students about the importance of giving clear, thorough written explanations of their thinking. Specific motivation techniques and suggestions for developing mathematical communication skills are included in the *Advanced Common Core Math Explorations: A Teacher's Guide* e-booklet.

Follow Up

The level of challenge in these explorations makes it impractical for most students to complete them entirely on their own as seatwork or homework. Students' most meaningful (and enjoyable!) experiences are often the opportunities you give them to have mathematical conversations with you and with each other while the activity is in progress. If you are implementing an activity with a small group of students in a mainstream classroom, it may be sufficient to plan to meet with them a couple of times per week, for 15 or 20 minutes each time. If circumstances allow more time than this, then the conversations and learning can be still better.

The Teacher's Guide for each exploration reprints each problem and contains two main elements: (a) Questions and Conversations and (b) Solution. The Questions and Conversations feature is designed to help you facilitate these conversations with and among students. For the most part, it lists questions that students may ask or that you may pose to them. Ideas for responding to the questions are included. It isn't necessary to ask or answer all of the questions. Instead, let students' ideas and your experience and professional judgment determine the flow of the conversation. The Solution section offers ideas for follow-up discussions with students as they work. Although the answers in the Questions and Conversations sections are often intentionally incomplete or suggestive of ideas to consider, you'll find detailed answers, often with samples of multiple approaches that students pursue in the Solution section.

Summarize

After students have finished an exploration, plan a brief discussion (20 minutes is usually enough) to give them a chance to share and critique one another's ideas and strategies. This is also a good time to answer any remaining questions they have. The Wrap Up section at the end of each exploration offers ideas for this discussion, along with suggestions for further exploration.

Assess

One of the most valuable things you can do for your students is to comment on their work. You don't have to write a lot, but your comments should show that you have read and thought about what they have written. Whether you give praise or offer suggestions for growth, make your comments specific and sincere. Ideally, some of your comments will relate to the detail of the mathematical content. Some specific suggestions are included in the free e-booklet accompanying this series.

If you would like to give students a numerical score, consider using a rubric such as the one in *Extending the Challenge in Mathematics: Developing Mathematical Promise in K–8 Students* (Sheffield, 2003). Whatever system you use, the emphasis should be on process goals such as problem solving, reasoning, communication, and making connections—not just correct answers. You may also build in general criteria such as effort, perseverance, correct spelling and grammar, organization, legibility, etc. However, remember that the central goal is to develop students' mathematical capacity. Any scoring system should reflect this.

GETTING STARTED

Here are some tips for getting started. First, a few "DON'Ts" to help you avoid some common pitfalls:

» *Don't feel that you have to finish the activities.* Students will learn more from thinking deeply about one or two questions than from rushing to finish an activity. Each exploration is designed to contain problems that will challenge virtually any student. Most students will not be able to answer every question.

» *Don't feel that you have to explain everything to students.* Your most important job is to help them learn to develop and test their own ideas. They will learn more if they do most of the thinking.

» *Don't be afraid to allow students to struggle.* Talented students need to know that meaningful learning takes time and hard work. Many of them need to experience some frustration—and learn to manage it.

» *Don't feel that you have to know all of the answers.* In order to challenge our students mathematically, we have to do the same for ourselves. You'll never know all of the answers, but if you're like me, you'll learn more about the math every time you teach an exploration! Do what you can during the time you've allotted to prepare, and then allow yourself to learn from the mathematical conversations—right along with your students.

And now some important "DOs":

» *Take your time.* Allow the students plenty of time to think about the problems. Take the time to explore the ideas in depth rather than rushing to get to the next question.

» *Play with the mathematics!* To many people's surprise, math is very much about creative play. Of course, there are learning goals, and it takes effort, but also be sure to enjoy playing with the patterns, numbers, shapes, and ideas!

» *Listen closely to students' ideas and expect them to listen closely to each other.* Meaningful mathematical conversation may be the single most important key to students' learning. It is also your key to assessing their learning.

» *Help students feel comfortable taking risks.* When you place less emphasis on the answers and show more interest in the quality of students' engagement, ideas, creativity, and questions, they will feel freer to make mistakes and grow from them.

» *Believe that the students—and you—can do it!* Middle school students have great success with these activities, but it may take some time to adjust to the level of challenge.

» *Use the explorations flexibly.* You don't always have to use them exactly "as is." Feel free to insert, delete, or modify questions to meet your students' needs. Adjust due dates or completion goals as necessary based on your observations of students.

Teachers who use the activities in a mainstream classroom often find it helpful to make a solid but realistic commitment at the beginning of the school year to implement the explorations. Put together a general plan for selecting students, forming groups, creating time for students to work (including time for you to meet with them), assessing the activities, and communicating with parents. Stick with your basic plan, making adjustments as needed as the school year progresses.

THE E-BOOKLET

The Advanced Common Core Math Explorations series comes with a free e-booklet (see http://www.prufrock.com/Assets/ClientPages/AdvancedCCMath. aspx) that contains detailed suggestions and tools for bringing the activities to life in your classroom. It addresses topics such as motivation, questioning techniques, mathematical communication, assessment, parent communication, implementing the explorations in different settings, and identification.

Connections to the Common Core State Standards

COMMON CORE STATE STANDARDS FOR MATHEMATICAL CONTENT

Table 1 outlines connections between the activities in *Advanced Common Core Math Explorations: Numbers and Operations* and the Common Core State Standards for Mathematics (NGA & CCSSO, 2010). The Standard column lists the CCSS Mathematics Content standards that apply to the activity. The Connections column shows other standards that are also addressed in the exploration. Extending the Core Learning describes how the activity extends student learning relative to the listed standard(s).

COMMON CORE STATE STANDARDS FOR MATHEMATICAL PRACTICE

The Common Core State Standards for Mathematical Practice are central to the purpose and structure of the activities in *Advanced Common Core Math Explorations: Numbers and Operations*. The list below outlines the ways in which the activities are built around these standards, providing a few specific examples for purposes of illustration.

1. **Make sense of problems and persevere in solving them.** All of the explorations in the *Advanced Common Core Math Explorations: Numbers and Operations* book engage students in understanding and solving problems. The process begins when you introduce the activity to your students and have a discussion in which everyone works together to clarify the meaning of the question and think about how to begin. Throughout each exploration, students devise problem-solving strategies, and make and test conjectures to guide their decisions and evaluate their progress as they work. They use visual models such as number lines (in a variety of forms) and Base Ten blocks, and they create and analyze stories based on real-life situations to help them develop a deep understanding of the underlying concepts. To promote perseverance, the activities have a high level of cognitive demand, and there is support for the teacher and students in the form of motivation strategies, a tiered structure for the explorations, and suggestions for facilitating mathematical conversation.

TABLE 1

Alignment With Common Core State Standards for Mathematical Content

	Exploration	Standard	Connections	Extending the Core Learning
1.	Triangle Sums	5.NBT.B.5–7	5.OA.A 5.OA.B	Use a whole number computation problem to learn about the mathematical investigation process.
2.	Torran Math	5.NBT.A.1	5.OA.B	Explore place value systems built on groupings (bases) other than Base Ten.
3.	Number Line Magnifiers	5.NBT.A.1 5.NBT.A.3 5.NBT.A.4 5.NBT.B.7		Extend the number line model to compare, round, compute, explore precision, and create stories with decimals to any place value.
4.	Million, Billion, Trillion . . .	5.NBT.A.1 5.NBT.A.2 8.EE.A.1–4	5.MD.A.1	Understand scientific notation using the order of magnitude concept. Solve problems and reason about size relationships between very large numbers.
5.	Discovering Divisibility Tests	5.NBT.A.1	4.OA.B.4 6.EE.A.2	Understand the role of place value in divisibility tests. Apply these concepts to create new tests.
6.	Visualizing Decimal Multiplication	5.NBT.B.7 6.NS.B.3	6.EE.A.2	Learn a variety of decimal multiplication strategies and use visual models to analyze connections between them.
7.	Think Like a Torran!	5.NBT.A.1–4 5.NBT.B.5–7		Create and justify computational algorithms and represent numbers less than 1 in a different place value system.
8.	Extreme Calculations	5.NBT.A.1 5.NBT.A.2 8.EE.A.1–4	5.MD.A.1	Create, justify, and apply computational strategies for working with very small and very large numbers. Reason about properties of integer exponents.
9.	Multiplication Slide Rules	6.NS.C.6 8.EE.A.1–4	5.NBT.A.1–4 7.NS.A.1 8.NS.A.2	Analyze and extend complex patterns in a number line model to deepen understanding of place value and powers of 10.
10.	Factor Blocks and Radicals	7.EE.A 8.EE.A.1 8.EE.A.2	6.NS.B.4 6.EE.A.2	Use a visual model to discover connections between radicals and noninteger exponents and to generate equivalent numeric and algebraic expressions.

2. **Reason abstractly and quantitatively.** The activities in this book provide students with frequent opportunities to understand and investigate connections between mathematical concepts and quantities. For example in "Torran Math" and "Think Like a Torran," students explore the effects on counting and computation when you choose a different base for place value groups. In "Multiplication Slide Rules," they examine relationships between two different types of number scales and explore connections to exponents. And in "Divisibility Tests," they observe the role of place value in creating tests for divisibility, and then use this knowledge to develop new tests.

3. **Construct viable arguments and critique the reasoning of others.** These activities often prompt students to use what they have learned in earlier questions or explorations to justify a conclusion or explain why a new fact must be true. For example, in "Triangle Sums," students analyze different solutions to a problem to determine what they have in common, how many of them there are, and why their conclusions make sense. In "Million, Billion, Trillion" and "Extreme Calculations," students explain what causes various patterns when calculating with powers of 10. And in "Factor Blocks and Radicals," students make and test conjectures about the meaning of representations of radicals and justify the conclusions that they reach. The "Questions and Conversations" and "Wrap Up" features in each exploration provide ongoing support for the teacher to lead discussions in which students compare and critique strategies and arguments of others.

4. **Model with mathematics.** In "Number Line Magnifiers" and "Visualizing Decimal Multiplication," students create stories and questions to model real-life situations and make approximations to help them form conclusions. In "Million, Billion, Trillion" and "Extreme Calculations," they apply computational tools to physical situations to develop a feel for the sizes of numbers and then interpret their results in the context of the situations.

5. **Use appropriate tools strategically.** Throughout these explorations, students develop and use a set of tools to solve problems and analyze mathematical concepts, including number lines and rulers, drawings of place value blocks, and a "building blocks" model for factors. Students make choices about the appropriateness of using mental math, paper and pencil, or calculators for computations with large numbers and powers of 10.

6. **Attend to precision.** Students are consistently expected to give clear and complete explanations of strategies and procedures using appropriate vocabulary. In many of the activities, especially in "Million, Billion, Trillion" and "Extreme Calculations," they state units of measure in their calculations and pay attention to the level of precision in their results, assuring that it is appropriate to the situation. Teachers are provided with support for leading discussions that develop students' communication skills. A section in the e-booklet accompanying the series is devoted to helping stu-

dents understand why it is important to communicate clearly and precisely and how to do so effectively.

7. **Look for and make use of structure.** Pattern and structure are central components of the explorations in *Advanced Common Core Math Explorations: Numbers and Operations.* In some activities, students analyze the structure of our Base Ten place value system and use it to design and justify computational strategies and algorithms, to develop divisibility tests, and to generalize the structure to other bases. In other activities, they look for patterns in the behavior of exponents as they perform calculations, using these to develop new and more efficient procedures, or to write equivalent expressions based on visual models. They regularly stop to evaluate what they are doing as they work, shifting perspectives to gain new understandings. For example, in "Divisibility Tests," they use their experience with previous tests to modify their representations of numbers and procedures as the tests become more complex. And in "Visualizing Decimal Multiplication," they continuously relate new algorithms to older ones, considering the ways in which they contain the same information in different forms.

8. **Look for and express regularity in repeated reasoning.** In *Advanced Common Core Math Explorations: Numbers and Operations*, students are constantly engaged in calculations and processes that display regularity. They use this predictability to find more efficient procedures, develop equations, and probe connections between concepts. For example, in "Think Like a Torran," students look for regularity in the changing appearances of numerals as they multiply and divide by 4 and 2. They use their observations to develop more efficient procedures and understand the role that place value plays in these patterns. In "Multiplication Slide Rules," students use patterns in distances between numbers to extend a scale beyond the interval between 0 and 1. They finish by generating an equation to describe the relationship between two scales.

Exploration **1**

Triangle Sums

INTRODUCTION

Prior Knowledge

» Add, subtract, multiply and divide one- and two-digit numbers.

Learning Goals

» Experience a mathematical investigation process.
» Develop and flexibly apply problem-solving strategies.
» Analyze and extend patterns.
» Make and test mathematical conjectures.
» Justify conclusions using deductive reasoning.
» Formulate questions and generalize solutions.
» Communicate complex mathematical ideas clearly.
» Persist in solving challenging problems.

Launching the Exploration

Motivation and purpose. To students: This exploration is an extended version of an entertaining puzzle that has been around for years. Its main purpose is to introduce you to the process that mathematicians use to discover and create new mathematical knowledge. You will gather information, organize it, analyze it, make predictions, test them, try to prove (or disprove!) your conclusions, and then create new questions to explore. In the process, you will strengthen your computational, problem-solving, and mathematical reasoning skills.

Understanding the problem. Read through the first question to ensure that students understand it. Emphasize the fact that each number must be used exactly once—none of them will be left out or repeated.

Encourage students to begin the exploration using "thinking paper." This is a place where they record their ideas, calculations, conjectures, and observations—essentially everything they do—as they work. They should save this paper and use it to help them write their final copy.

Some students may enjoy cutting out nine circles, numbering them, and moving them around as they try to solve the puzzle. However, remind them that they should still keep track of their work on the thinking paper.

STUDENT HANDOUT

Stage 1

1. Use each of the numbers 1, 2, 3, 4, 5, 6, 7, 8, and 9 exactly once to fill in the circles. Make the sum of each side equal to 17. Describe your thinking strategies.

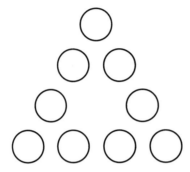

2. Find a different solution to the problem.

3. What important feature do your solutions have in common?

4. How can you see that these are the only two solutions?

Stage 2

5. Add the counting numbers 1 through 9. Then calculate $17 \cdot 3$. How does this relate to the original Triangle Sums problem? Why aren't the two answers the same?

6. Why must your two solutions have the common feature you described in Problem #3? How does this show you another way to see that there are only two solutions? Explain.

7. Fill in the circles with the numbers 1, 2, 3, 4, 5, 6, 7, 8, and 9 as before. Try to make the three sides have the same sum, but this time larger than 17!

8. Why can't "Triangle Sums" be solved for a sum smaller than 17? Explain.

9. Suppose you have a triangle with five circles on each side instead of four. Using the numbers 1–12, what is the smallest sum that will allow a solution to the problem? Explain your thinking.

10. Solve the new problem using this sum.

11. Imagine triangles with more and more circles on each side. Describe a method for finding the smallest sum that will allow a solution, no matter how many circles are on each side of the triangle.

12. Complete a table showing the smallest sum for triangles with 3, 4, 5, 6, and 7 circles per side.

13. Discover and describe a pattern in the smallest sums. Use your pattern to predict the next three sums.

14. Think of at least three more questions to extend the "Triangle Sums" exploration.

TEACHER'S GUIDE

STAGE 1

Problem #1

1. Use each of the numbers 1, 2, 3, 4, 5, 6, 7, 8, and 9 exactly once to fill in the circles. Make the sum of each side equal to 17. Describe your thinking strategies.

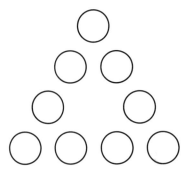

Questions and Conversations for #1

This section contains ideas for conversations, mainly in the form of questions that students may ask or that you may pose to them. Be sure to allow students to do most of the thinking and talking!

» *What might cause the sums to be too large?* Putting large numbers on the same side of the triangle or in the corners causes a problem. Can you see why?

» *How can you use unsuccessful attempts to move you toward a correct solution?* Rather than starting over when something doesn't work, change your earlier attempts one small step at a time, paying attention to how each change affects the sums.

» *How many ways can you make a sum of 17 with four numbers from 1 through 9?* This might be worth investigating. It helps organize your work and limits the number of things you have to try. It might also help you to find more solutions later, and to know when you've found all of them.

» *How can you explain your thinking process if it feels like you just tried numbers randomly until you found something that worked?* You may feel that you chose numbers randomly, but you almost certainly made choices along the way. Did you notice that your sums were too large? Did you make a plan to fix this problem? Did you keep track of things you had already tried? Did you list different ways to make sums of 17? Did you make small adjustments when you were close to a solution?

Solution for #1

A sample solution is:

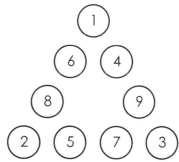

Sample student responses:

»   Avoid putting large numbers together on the same side of the triangle.

»   Notice that placing large numbers in the corners makes the sums too large (because these numbers are used more than once in the sums). Try smaller numbers in the corners.

»   Use a guess, check, and revise strategy. Put numbers in randomly, add the sides, and then make adjustments by switching pairs of numbers in order to raise some sums and lower others.

»   Find sets of four numbers that add to 17 (like 1, 2, 5, 9 and 1, 2, 6, 8 for example). Then find ways to fit them together into the triangle.

»   Notice that when you find sets of four numbers that add to 17, the numbers 1, 2, and 3 appear more often than others. This means that 1, 2, and 3 should be in the corners.

Problem #2

2. Find a different solution to the problem.

Questions and Conversations for #2

»   *What counts as a different solution?* You can decide, but most people agree that rotating or reflecting a solution, or interchanging two numbers in the middle of a side does not count as a new solution. This is what we mean when we say that there are only two solutions.

Solution for #2

Another sample solution is:

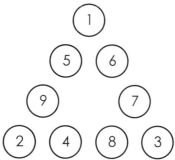

Problem #3

3. What important feature do your solutions have in common?

Questions and Conversations for #3

» *Where are the most important circles in the triangle? Why?* The most important circles are the ones in the corners, because each of them contributes to two of the sums.

» *Can you use your original solution to help you find a new one?* Possibly—if you pay attention to what should stay the same and what can change.

Solution for #3

In both solutions, the numbers 1, 2, and 3 are in the corners of the triangle.

Problem #4

4. How can you see that these are the only two solutions?

Questions and Conversations for #4

» *What happens to a solution if you exchange a corner number with one of the two middle numbers on any side?* It will always change one of the sums, making it greater than 17.

Solution for #4

Once you have a solution with 1, 2, and 3 in the corners, if you trade a corner number with a noncorner number (which will always be greater than 3), the sum of one or both sides touching that corner becomes greater than 17, ruining the solution! (What happens if you trade two corner numbers?)

STAGE 2

Problem #5

5. Add the counting numbers 1 through 9. Then calculate $17 \cdot 3$. How does this relate to the original Triangle Sums problem? Why aren't the two answers the same?

Questions and Conversations for #5

» *How do the answers to the two calculations compare? What causes this?* The two answers differ by 6. Why? Think about how this relates to the most important circles in the triangle.

Solution for #5

$$1+2+3+4+5+6+7+8+9 = 45 \qquad 17 \cdot 3 = 51$$

The equation on the left shows the sum of all of the numbers you place in the circles. The product on the right comes from adding the sums of the three sides of the triangle. The answers aren't the same because when you add these sums, you count each corner twice.

Problem #6

6. Why must your two solutions have the common feature you described in Problem #3? How does this show you another way to see that there are only two solutions? Explain.

Questions and Conversations for #6

See Questions and Conversations for #5.

Solution for #6

The corners must account for the difference of 6 between 45 and 51. The only way you can make the corners add to 6 is to place the numbers 1, 2, and 3 in them.

Because 1, 2, and 3 are in the corners, your choices for placing the remaining numbers are limited:

» The side containing 1 and 2 needs 14 more.
» The side containing 1 and 3 needs 13 more.
» The side containing 2 and 3 needs 12 more.

There are only two ways to accomplish this using the remaining six numbers:

$14 = 5 + 9$	$13 = 6 + 7$	$12 = 4 + 8$
$14 = 6 + 8$	$13 = 4 + 9$	$12 = 5 + 7$

Problem #7

7. Fill in the circles with the numbers 1, 2, 3, 4, 5, 6, 7, 8, and 9 as before. Try to make the three sides have the same sum, but this time larger than 17!

Solution for #7

A sample solution (this one happens to have the largest possible sum, 23):

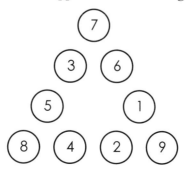

Problem #8

8. Why can't "Triangle Sums" be solved for a sum smaller than 17? Explain.

Questions and Conversations for #8

» *What would have to happen with the corners?* They would have to have smaller numbers in them.

Solution for #8

You obtain the smallest sum by using the smallest possible numbers in the corners. Because 1, 2, and 3 are the smallest numbers available, you can't form a sum smaller than 17.

STAGE 3

Problem #9

9. Suppose you have a triangle with five circles on each side instead of four. Using the numbers 1–12, what is the smallest sum that will allow a solution to the problem? Explain your thinking.

Questions and Conversations for #9

» *What numbers must be in the corners in order to achieve the lowest sum?* As before, the corners must hold the numbers 1, 2, and 3.

» *How should three times the sum of each side relate to the sum of the counting numbers in the circles?* The values in the corners can help you answer this question.

Solution for #9

The smallest sum is 28.

$$1+2+3+4+5+6+7+8+9+10+11+12 = 78$$

When you make the smallest sum, you must place 1, 2, and 3 in the corners. Because the corners must still have a sum of 6, you add $78 + 6 = 84$. (This counts each corner twice.) The three sums must add to 84, so the sum for each side is $84 \div 3 = 28$.

Problem #10

10. Solve the new problem using this sum.

Questions and Conversations for #10

See Questions and Conversations for #9.

Solution for #10

A sample solution:

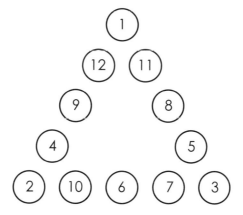

Problem #11

11. Imagine triangles with more and more circles on each side. Describe a method for finding the smallest sum that will allow a solution, no matter how many circles are on each side of the triangle.

Questions and Conversations for #11

See Questions and Conversations for #9.

Solution for #11

Follow the same process we used above. Count the number of circles in the triangle. Add all of the counting numbers from 1 through this number. Add 6 to this total and then divide the result by 3.

Problem #12

12. Complete a table showing the smallest sum for triangles with 3, 4, 5, 6, and 7 circles per side.

Solution for #12

Number of Circles Per Side	Smallest Sum for a Solution
3	9
4	17
5	28
6	42
7	59

Problem #13

13. Discover and describe a pattern in the smallest sums. Use your pattern to predict the next three sums.

Questions and Conversations for #13

» *How do you get from one number to the next for the list of smallest sums in your table?* Focus on the differences between the numbers.

Solution for #13

The "smallest sum" seems to be increasing by 8, 11, 14 and then 17. The difference is increasing by 3 each time. If this pattern continues, the smallest sums will be

$59 + 20 = 79$	for 8 circles
$79 + 23 = 102$	for 9 circles
$102 + 26 = 128$	for 10 circles

Problem #14

14. Think of at least three more questions to extend the "Triangle Sums" exploration.

Questions and Conversations for #14

» *Were there any questions that arose in your mind as you were working? Is there anything you were curious about?* Answers will vary.
» *We adjusted the number of circles per side. What other things might you change?* You could change the basic shape from a triangle to something else. You could try a different operation than addition. You might try placing different kinds of numbers in the circles.

Solution for #14

See the "Further Exploration" feature at the end of this activity for some ideas.

WRAP UP

Share Strategies

Have students share their strategies and compare results.

Summarize

Answer any remaining questions that students have. Summarize a typical mathematical exploration process:

» ask a question;

» explore—gather information and search for strategies;

» organize and analyze the information, look for patterns;

» make conjectures or predictions;

» test the conjectures;

» prove the conjectures or try to understand why they are (or are not) true; and

» reflect on what you've learned and think of new questions to ask.

Help students see how "Triangle Sums" fits this pattern of mathematical exploration. Encourage them to remain aware of this process in future explorations. At the same time, make sure they understand that no single list can capture the true nature of what it means to "do mathematics." You will sometimes leave out some of these steps, incorporate different ones, or do them in a different order.

Further Exploration

Ask students to think of ways to continue or extend this exploration. Here are some possibilities:

» Are there patterns in the largest possible sums for solutions? How do they relate to the smallest sums?

» Is it possible to solve the problem for each whole number between the smallest and largest possible sums?

» What happens if you use squares instead of triangles?

» What happens if the sides must have the same product?

» How many solutions will the original problem have if it does count as a new solution when you rotate or reflect the original triangle or exchange the numbers in the middle of a side? (Answer: 96)

» Can you find a formula for the relationship in the table from Problem #12? (Sample answer: $y = \frac{1}{2}\left(3x^2 - 5x + 6\right)$ where x represents the number of circles per side, and y stands for the smallest sum.) This will be a big challenge because most students won't know formal algebraic procedures, but never underestimate what a determined student can accomplish! Those who do have more background in algebra might try to derive the formula from the problem situation.

Exploration 2

Torran Math

Prior Knowledge

» Understand how place value is used to represent numbers.
» Understand the role of place value in procedures for whole number addition, subtraction, multiplication, and division.

Learning Goals

» Deepen understanding of place value by exploring a system that groups by a number other than 10.
» Develop, describe, and justify procedures for translating between two place value systems.
» Analyze and extend counting patterns in a new place value system.
» Understand the difference between numbers (ideas) and numerals (symbols).
» Communicate complex mathematical ideas clearly.
» Persist in solving challenging problems.

Launching the Exploration

Motivation and purpose. To students: One of the best ways to better understand your own language is to learn someone else's. In the same way, if you want to gain a deeper understanding of your own numeration system, it helps to study a different system! To do this, you will visit the imaginary planet, Torr, where they group everything by fours instead of tens. As you investigate the Torran way of writing numerals, pay close attention to the similarities and differences between our systems.

Understanding the problem. Ask students to read the first page of the activity very carefully. Have them discuss what they've learned and what they are still trying to understand. (They should not feel that they have to understand everything right now.) Encourage students to refer to the first page whenever they feel confused or get stuck.

Discuss the distinction between *numbers* and *numerals*. Tell students to stay focused on this distinction throughout the exploration.

Don't explain anything beyond the content of the introductory page. Especially do not teach explicit procedures for translating between the Earth and Torran numeration systems. Students will develop their own strategies based upon their own understandings.

Teacher's Note. Even though this exploration is about different number *base* systems, notice that we never use the word *base*. This is to encourage students to think as independently as possible and avoid the temptation to "look it up." You might like to introduce the term at the end of the exploration.

STUDENT HANDOUT

You are part of an expedition to the planet Torr. The Torrans have only two fingers on each hand! Because of this, their place value system uses groups of four instead of ten. Your job is to figure out how they write their numerals. So far, your investigations have turned up the following mysterious relationships between our numerals and the Torran numerals.

Our Numeral	Torran Numeral
8	20
11	23
15	33
19	103

When we write "23," it means "2 groups of ten and 3 ones,"

Tens	Ones
2	3

which represents *twenty-three* objects. We would group them like this:

xxxxxxxxxx xxxxxxxxxx xxx

But when the Torrans write "23," it means "2 groups of four and 3 ones,"

Fours	Ones
2	3

which represents *eleven* objects. They would group them like this:

xxxx xxxx xxx

Notice how the Torrans make groups of four instead of ten.

This may seem strange to you, so think about it for a while before you begin the exploration. It helps to understand the difference between a *number* and a *numeral*.

A *number* is an idea that tells you how many or how much. A *numeral* is a symbol (or set of symbols) that we use to write the number. Different cultures may use different numerals to represent the same number. The numeral "23" means something different to us than it does to the Torrans. For us, "23" represents a count or measure of *twenty-three*. For the Torrans, "23" represents a count or measure of *eleven*!

In this activity, when we use a numeral in a sentence, we will put it in quotes. Numbers will be usually shown in *italics* (unless they describe a place value). Also, we will often write numbers in word form so that they don't look like numerals.

Stage 1

1. Our numeral for the number *eight* is "8," which means 8 ones. But your investigations have shown that the Torrans write the numeral for *eight* as "20." Draw *eight* x's and show how the Torrans would group them. Use your diagram to explain why the Torrans write *eight* as "20."

2. Our numeral for *fifteen* is "15," which means 1 group of ten and 5 ones. Your investigations have shown that the Torrans write the numeral for *fifteen* as "33." Draw *fifteen* x's and show how the Torrans would group them. Use your diagram to explain why the Torrans write *fifteen* as "33."

3. Our smallest whole number place values are the ones and the tens. The next place value is hundreds. The Torrans' smallest whole number place values are the ones and the fours. What is their next place value? Explain.

4. Use your answer from the last question to explain why the Torrans write *nineteen* as "103."

5. We would use place value blocks to show the number *two hundred forty-six* as

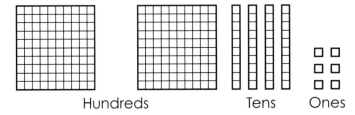

Hundreds   Tens   Ones

   This diagram shows 2 flats (groups of one hundred) plus 4 longs (groups of ten) plus 6 smalls (groups of one). How would the Torrans use their place value blocks to show their numeral "103" (see Problem #4)? Explain how your diagram shows that the Torran numeral "103" represents *nineteen*.

6. Draw a picture showing how Torrans would use their place value blocks to represent *forty-one*. How would the Torrans write the numeral for this number? Use your place value block picture to help you explain your answer.

7. What is the fourth Torran place value? Explain your thinking.

8. The Torran numeral for *ninety-nine* is "1203." Explain why.

9. What would the Torran numeral for *one hundred ninety-seven* look like? Explain.

10. You may have noticed that the Torran numerals contain only the digits 0, 1, 2, and 3! Use Torran place value to explain why they would never use the digit 4 (or any larger digit).

11. The Torran numeral for some number is "12031." What number does this represent? How would we write its numeral on Earth? Show your work and explain.

12. Make a table to show the Torran numerals for the numbers *one* through *seventy-five*. The left column should contain our numerals for these numbers. The right column should contain the corresponding Torran numerals.

On Earth, the ancient Mayans often grouped by 20, while the Mesopotamians formed groups of 60. (We still sometimes do this today! When?) On Torr, there is a culture, called the Omera, that groups by two.

13. Make a table showing the Torran and the Omeran numerals for the numbers *twenty-one*, *forty-two*, *sixty-three*, and *two hundred twenty-eight*. Show your work to find the Omeran numeral for *two hundred twenty-eight*.

14. Create a quick procedure for translating directly from Torran to Omeran numerals (without turning them into Earth numerals in between). Give at least one example.

15. Create a quick procedure for translating directly from Omeran to Torran numerals.

16. Imagine a culture that uses groups of sixteen for their numeration system! How many symbols will they need? Why? Create any new symbols that are needed and use them to show how to write the numbers *fifty-eight* and *seven hundred nine* in this numeration system.

TEACHER'S GUIDE

You are part of an expedition to the planet Torr. The Torrans have only two fingers on each hand! Because of this, their place value system uses groups of four instead of ten. Your job is to figure out how they write their numerals. So far, your investigations have turned up the following mysterious relationships between our numerals and the Torran numerals.

Our Numeral	Torran Numeral
8	20
11	23
15	33
19	103

When we write "23," it means "2 groups of ten and 3 ones,"

Tens	Ones
2	3

which represents *twenty-three* objects. We would group them like this:

xxxxxxxxxx xxxxxxxxxx xxx

But when the Torrans write "23," it means "2 groups of four and 3 ones,"

Fours	Ones
2	3

which represents *eleven* objects. They would group them like this:

xxxx xxxx xxx

Notice how the Torrans make groups of four instead of ten.

This may seem strange to you, so think about it for a while before you begin the exploration. It helps to understand the difference between a *number* and a *numeral*.

A *number* is an idea that tells you how many or how much. A *numeral* is a symbol (or set of symbols) that we use to write the number. Different cultures may use different numerals to represent the same number. The numeral "23" means something different to us than it does to the Torrans. For us, "23" represents a count or measure of *twenty-three*. For the Torrans, "23" represents a count or measure of *eleven*!

In this activity, when we use a numeral in a sentence, we will put it in quotes. Numbers will be usually shown in *italics* (unless they describe a place value). Also, we will often write numbers in word form so that they don't look like numerals.

STAGE 1

Problem #1

1. Our numeral for the number *eight* is "8," which means 8 ones. But your investigations have shown that the Torrans write the numeral for *eight* as "20." Draw *eight* x's and show how the Torrans would group them. Use your diagram to explain why the Torrans write *eight* as "20."

Teacher's Note for #1. As students begin having conversations about Torran grouping, the issue of how to read and speak the numerals will probably arise. For example, it would not be appropriate to read the Torran numeral "20" as "twenty" because twenty means "two groups of ten." For the numeral "103" (from Problem #4), the difficulty is even more obvious because we actually use the word "hundred" when we read it! Unfortunately, our language does not contain separate suffixes and words to describe groups of 4, 16, 64, etc. A common way to get around this issue is to speak these numerals by simply reading the digits. For example, we read the Torran numeral "20" as "two-zero," and "103" as "one-zero-three."

Solution for #1

The Torran numeral "20" represents 2 groups of four and 0 ones.

xxxx xxxx

Problem #2

2. Our numeral for *fifteen* is "15," which means 1 group of ten and 5 ones. Your investigations have shown that the Torrans write the numeral for *fifteen* as "33." Draw *fifteen* x's and show how the Torrans would group them. Use your diagram to explain why the Torrans write *fifteen* as "33."

Solution for #2

The Torran numeral "33" represents 3 groups of four and 3 ones.

xxxx xxxx xxxx xxx

Problem #3

3. Our smallest whole number place values are the ones and the tens. The next place value is hundreds. The Torrans' smallest whole number place values are the ones and the fours. What is their next place value? Explain.

Questions and Conversations for #3

This section contains ideas for conversations, mainly in the form of questions that students may ask or that you may pose to them. Be sure to allow students to do most of the thinking and talking!

» *Why is the answer not "forties"?* The answer is not "forties" because forty is 10 groups of four, and the Torrans do not use tens to create place value groups.

» *If we make hundreds using 10 groups of ten, how do the Torrans make their next place value?* Just follow the pattern—but remember that Torrans don't use groups of ten!

Solution for #3

Because the Torrans group everything by fours, the next place value group is 4 groups of four, or sixteen.

Problem #4

4. Use your answer from the last question to explain why the Torrans write *nineteen* as "103."

Questions and Conversations for #4

» *If the "3" represents 3 groups of one; the "0" represents 0 groups of four, what does the "1" represent?* It stands for 1 group of the new place value you found in Problem #3!

Solution for #4

The numeral "103" stands for 1 group of sixteen, 0 groups of four, and 3 groups of one. This is a total of *nineteen*.

Problem #5

5. We would use place value blocks to show the number *two hundred forty-six* as

This diagram shows 2 flats (groups of one hundred) plus 4 longs (groups of ten) plus 6 smalls (groups of one). How would the Torrans use their place value blocks to show their numeral "103" (see Problem #4)?

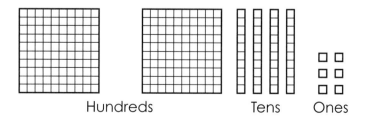

Hundreds   Tens Ones

Explain how your diagram shows that the Torran numeral "103" represents *nineteen*.

Questions and Conversations for #5

» *How many blocks will be in a Torran small? Long? Flat?* The smalls still stand for one. Try to build the longs and flats the same way we do, using groups of four instead of ten.

Solution for #5

This diagram shows 1 flat (sixteen), 0 longs (fours) and 3 smalls (ones), which makes a total of nineteen.

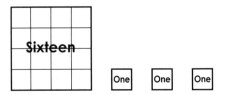

Problem #6

6. Draw a picture showing how Torrans would use their place value blocks to represent *forty-one*. How would the Torrans write the numeral for this number? Use your place value block picture to help you explain your answer.

Questions and Conversations for #6

See Questions and Conversations for #5.

Solution for #6

Torrans would write *forty-one* as "221." This represents 2 flats (groups of sixteen), 2 longs (groups of four) and 1 small (one). The total number of blocks is *forty-one*.

STAGE 2

Problem #7

7. What is the fourth Torran place value? Explain your thinking.

Questions and Conversations for #7

» *How do Torrans get to the next higher place value?* On Earth, we multiply by ten. Look for a pattern in the Torran place values that you've already found.

Solution for #7

Sample student response 1: The fourth place value is sixty-four. In our system, each place value group is ten times larger than the previous one. For the Torrans, each place value is four times larger than the previous one. Sixteen times four is sixty-four.

Sample student response 2: The fourth place value is sixty-four. The large cube in Torran place value blocks has a length, width, and height of four blocks each. It contains a total of 64 small cubes.

Problem #8

8. The Torran numeral for *ninety-nine* is "1203." Explain why.

Questions and Conversations for #8

» *How many large cubes will the Torrans use to make* ninety-nine? *How many will remain?* They will use 1 large cube, which holds sixty-four smalls. Thirty-five smalls will remain.

Solution for #8

The Torran numeral "1203" represents 1 group of sixty-four, 2 groups of sixteen, 0 groups of four, and 3 groups of one. This makes a total of *ninety-nine*.

Problem #9

9. What would the Torran numeral for *one hundred ninety-seven* look like? Explain.

Questions and Conversations for #9

» *How many large cubes will the Torrans use to make* one hundred ninety-seven? *How many will remain?* They will use 3 large cubes, which accounts for $3 \cdot 64 = 192$ small blocks. Five smalls will remain.

Solution for #9

The Torran numeral for the number *one hundred ninety-seven* is "3011." Start with sixty-four—the largest place value less than *one hundred ninety-seven*.

Groups of sixty-four:	3	$3 \cdot 64 = 192$	Remaining:	$197 - 192 = 5$
Groups of sixteen:	0	$0 \cdot 16 = 0$	Remaining:	$5 - 0 = 5$
Groups of four:	1	$1 \cdot 4 = 4$	Remaining:	$5 - 4 = 1$
Groups of one:	1	$1 \cdot 1 = 1$	Remaining:	$1 - 1 = 0$

One hundred ninety-seven is 3 groups of sixty-four, 0 groups of sixteen, 1 group of four, and 1 group of 1. This is written "3011" in Torran.

Problem #10

10. You may have noticed that the Torran numerals contain only the digits 0, 1, 2, and 3! Use Torran place value to explain why they would never use the digit 4 (or any larger digit).

Questions and Conversations for #10

» *What would happen if the Torrans put a "4" in the fours column?* It would make a group of sixteen.

Solution for #10

If the Torrans used a digit equal to or greater than 4, it would form larger place value group and the numeral would have an extra digit.

Example: A 4 in the fours column would stand for 4 groups of four, but this is 1 group of sixteen. So instead of writing *sixteen* as "40," the Torrans would show it as "100."

Problem #11

11. The Torran numeral for some number is "12031." What number does this represent? How would we write its numeral on Earth? Show your work and explain.

Questions and Conversations for #11

» *What is different about this question?* You have to think backward. You are turning a Torran numeral into an Earth numeral.

Solution for #11

After sixty-four, the next Torran place value is two hundred fifty-six. "12031" stands for 1 group of two hundred fifty-six, 2 groups of sixty-four, 0 groups of sixteen, 3 groups of four, and 1 group of one.

$$1 \cdot 256 + 2 \cdot 64 + 0 \cdot 16 + 3 \cdot 4 + 1 \cdot 1$$

This is a total of *three hundred ninety-seven*, or in Earth numerals, "397."

Problem #12

12. Make a table to show the Torran numerals for the numbers *one* through *seventy-five*. The left column should contain our numerals for these numbers. The right column should contain the corresponding Torran numerals.

Questions and Conversations for #12

» *When will the first Torran three-digit numeral appear?* It will appear somewhere between *ten* and *twenty*.
» *When will the first Torran four-digit numeral appear?* It will appear somewhere between *sixty* and *seventy*.
» *If you use patterns in the numerals to help you count in Torran, how can you check your work as you go?* Every so often, you can use the strategies from earlier in this exploration to turn some of the Earth numerals into Torran numerals (or the reverse).

Solution for #12

Our Numeral	Torran Numeral	Our Numeral	Torran Numeral	Our Numeral	Torran Numeral
1	1	13	31	25	121
2	2	14	32	26	122
3	3	15	33	27	123
4	10	**16**	**100**	28	130
5	11	17	101	29	131
6	12	18	102	30	132
7	13	19	103	31	133
8	20	20	110	32	200
9	21	21	111	33	201
10	22	22	112	34	202
11	23	23	113	35	203
12	30	24	120	36	210

Our Numeral	Torran Numeral	Our Numeral	Torran Numeral	Our Numeral	Torran Numeral
37	211	50	302	63	333
38	212	51	303	**64**	**1000**
39	213	52	310	65	1001
40	220	53	311	66	1002
41	221	54	312	67	1003
42	222	55	313	68	1010
43	223	56	320	69	1011
44	230	57	321	70	1012
45	231	58	322	71	1013
46	232	59	323	72	1020
47	233	60	330	73	1021
48	300	61	331	74	1022
49	301	62	332	75	1023

STAGE 3

Problem #13

On Earth, the ancient Mayans often grouped by 20, while the Mesopotamians formed groups of 60. (We still sometimes do this today! When?) On Torr, there is a culture, called the Omera, that groups by two.

13. Make a table showing the Torran and the Omeran numerals for the numbers *twenty-one, forty-two, sixty-three,* and *two hundred twenty-eight.* Show your work to find the Omeran numeral for *two hundred twenty-eight.*

Questions and Conversations for #13

» *Is there a connection between the Torran and the Omeran place values?* Yes. The Torran place values are every second number in the list of Omeran place values.

Solution for #13

Number	Torran	Omeran
twenty-one	111	10101
forty-two	222	101010
sixty-three	333	111111
two hundred twenty-eight	3210	11100100

The Omeran place values are 1, 2, 4, 8, 16, 32, 64, 128, 256, etc. The largest one that is less than two hundred twenty-eight is one hundred twenty-eight. We'll form as many groups of each place as possible.

Groups	Amount Remaining
1 group of one hundred twenty-eight	100
1 group of sixty-four	36
1 group of thirty-two	4
0 groups of sixteen	4
0 groups of eight	4
1 group of four	0
0 groups of two	0
0 groups of one	0

Looking down the column showing the number of groups, we get 11100100.

Problem #14

14. Create a quick procedure for translating directly from Torran to Omeran numerals (without turning them into Earth numerals in between). Give at least one example.

Questions and Conversations for #14

» *Are there any patterns in the table from Problem #13 that might be helpful?* There are many patterns. Consider looking at one or two digits at a time.
» *What can you do if you don't have enough examples of Torran and Omeran numerals to see patterns or make predictions?* Create more examples of your own!

Solution for #14

For each digit in the Torran numeral, replace 0 by 00; replace 1 by 01; replace 2 by 10; and replace 3 by 11. If there is a 0 at the left end of the numeral, leave it off. For example, writing 3210 (Torran) as an Omeran numeral looks like this.

3	2	1	0
11	10	01	00

Problem #15

15. Create a quick procedure for translating directly from Omeran to Torran numerals.

Questions and Conversations for #15

See Questions and Conversations for #14.

Solution for #15

Reverse the process. Starting at the right end of the Omeran numeral, clump the digits into pairs. Then replace 00 by 0; replace 01 by 1; replace 10 by 2; and replace 11 by 3.

Here is what it looks like for the number *two hundred twenty-eight*.

Split 11100100 into pairs:	11	10	01	00
Replace each pair by the correct numeral:	3	2	1	0

Problem #16

16. Imagine a culture that uses groups of sixteen for their numeration system! How many symbols will they need? Why? Create any new symbols that are needed and use them to show how to write the numbers *fifty-eight* and *seven hundred nine* in this numeration system.

Questions and Conversations for #16

» *How many symbols do the Torrans use? How about the Omerans? How many do we use on Earth?* The Torrans use four symbols (0, 1, 2, and 3). The Omerans use two symbols (0 and 1). On Earth, we use 10 symbols (0, 1, 2, 3, 4, 5, 6, 7, 8, and 9).

» *Why can't the number* ten *be written as a two-digit numeral in a system based on groups of sixteen?* You need 16 ones to form the first complete place value group.

Solution for #16

The first 16 whole numbers must be represented by single-digit numerals. This means that you will need new symbols for *ten, eleven, twelve, thirteen, fourteen,* and *fifteen*.

You can create your own symbols for these if you like! Computer programmers, who often use a system based on groups of sixteen, just use letters.

$$10 \rightarrow A$$
$$11 \rightarrow B$$
$$12 \rightarrow C$$
$$13 \rightarrow D$$
$$14 \rightarrow E$$
$$15 \rightarrow F$$

Fifty-eight is written 3A because it contains 3 groups of sixteen and A (10) groups of one. If we check this using Earth numerals it looks like this:

$$3 \cdot 16 + 10 \cdot 1 = 58$$

Seven hundred nine is written 2C5, because it consists of 2 groups of two hundred fifty-six*, C (12) groups of sixteen, and 5 groups of one. Checking this with Earth numerals, we get:

$$2 \cdot 256 + 12 \cdot 16 + 5 \cdot 1 = 512 + 192 + 5 = 709$$

*Two hundred fifty-six is the third place value when you group by sixteens, because (using Earth numerals) $16 \cdot 16 = 256$.

WRAP UP

Share Strategies

Have students share their strategies and compare results.

Summarize

Answer any remaining questions that students have. Summarize a few key points and share some of this information:

» Numbers are ideas, and numerals are symbols that represent them. You can use different numerals to represent the same number. Roman numerals are a familiar example. For instance, 5 and V both stand for the same number, even though the numerals are different.

» One way to form numerals is to use groups to create a place value system. The Torran numeration system is known as a Base Four system because it is built on groups of four. We use a Base Ten system.

» The Base Two system of the Omerans is actually known as the *binary* system. On Earth, it forms the basis for computer calculations. Base Sixteen also has a special name, and it is used with computers as well. It is called the *hexadecimal* system.

Further Exploration

Ask students to think of ways to continue or extend this exploration. Here are some possibilities:

» The Torrans probably wouldn't actually use the same symbols that we do for the digits 0, 1, 2, and 3. Make up your own symbols and practice using them instead.

» Invent words for Torran numbers that reflect their place value system.

» Imagine Torran children learning math. How many single-digit facts would they have to memorize? Would their numerals generally be longer or shorter? What would their mental math "shortcuts" look like? How would their algorithms for the basic operations be similar to ours? How would they be different?

» Practice translating between Base Ten and other numeration systems such as Base Five or Base Six.

» Research the *hexadecimal* system. How is it used to name colors in computer graphics? How else is it used with computers?

» In Stage 3, you developed a procedure for translating directly between Base Two and Base Four. Can you create similar methods for translating between any other bases?

Exploration 3

Number Line Magnifiers

```
╲────────────────╱
  INTRODUCTION
╱────────────────╲
```

Materials

» Graph paper (optional—to draw number lines more easily and accurately)

Prior Knowledge

» Read and write decimals for numbers through hundredths or thousandths.
» Understand what it means to round a number to a given place value.

Learning Goals

» Visualize how each place value is related to the next by a factor of 10.
» Use place value flexibly to name small numbers (less than 1).
» Develop and justify visual procedures for comparing and rounding small numbers.
» Develop and justify visual procedures for adding and subtracting small numbers.
» Create real-world stories based on place value for small numbers.
» Begin to explore the idea of precision in small number measurements.
» Communicate complex mathematical ideas clearly.
» Persist in solving challenging problems.

> **Teacher's Note.** Students don't have to know procedures for comparing, rounding, adding, or subtracting decimals. They can develop their own strategies for these.

Launching the Exploration

Motivation and purpose. To students: One of the best ways to really understand a math concept is to visualize it, but this can be challenging when it comes to very small numbers. Fortunately, there is a clever "trick" you can use to help you picture how these numbers fit on a number line. It involves an imaginary magnifying glass—and you can use it to help you compare, round, add, and subtract numbers of all sizes!

Understanding the problem. Look through the entire exploration with students to help them get the big picture. They will be using number lines to visualize decimal concepts and processes. If they've already learned procedures for comparing rounding, adding, and subtracting decimals, challenge them to pretend that they don't know them yet. They may be able to get by without them altogether!

Discuss the terms *interval* and *operation* in the context of this activity.

Remind students that this exploration is not about speedy computation. It's about using visualization to develop a deeper understanding of small numbers.

STUDENT HANDOUT

Stage 1

1. This number line shows one unit. Copy it and label each dot with the correct decimal.

   a. What happens if you split each of the 10 parts into 10 parts again? What if you continue doing this?

   b. Place a small dot on the line as close as you can to 0.73 units. Explain your thinking.

2. Explain why 0.7, 0.70, and 0.700 all name the same number.

3. This diagram shows a "number line magnifier"—a magnified view of the interval between two dots on the main number line.

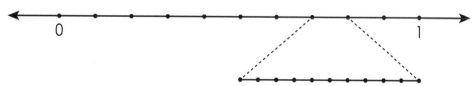

   a. Copy the diagram. Label the main number line as "tenths." Then label the magnifier with the appropriate place value name.

   b. Mark the numbers 0.73, 0.736 and 0.7368, adding more number line magnifiers as needed. Label each new magnifier with its place value name. Add more digits and more magnifiers if you like!

4. You can use place value to name numbers in many ways. For example, some ways to name 473 are:

     473 ones   47 tens and 3 ones   4 hundreds, 7 tens, and 3 ones

How could you could name 473 using tenths as one of the place values? Explain your thinking. (There are many possibilities.)

5. Write at least three ways to use place value to name the number 0.73.

6. Write at least five ways to use place value to name the number 0.736.

Stage 2

7. Explain how you can use your diagram from Problem #3 to round 0.7368 to the nearest thousandth, hundredth, tenth, and whole number.

8. Explain how you can use your number line diagram to answer these two questions.
   a. Which is greater, 0.7368 or 0.9?

   b. Which is greater, 0.7368 or 0.72?

9. Draw a number line with two magnifiers to show 0.163. Show how to use your diagram to move 0.702 units to the right of 0.163. Create and solve a real-world story to match this situation.

10. Draw a magnifier diagram that shows 0.9 and 0.58. Explain how to use your diagram to show how far apart these numbers are. Create and solve a real-world story to match this situation.

11. Why might it be harder to create a realistic story using the numbers 0.9 and 0.58114 (instead of 0.9 and 0.58)?

Stage 3

12. Draw a number line magnifier diagram that shows 0.27 and 0.6. Describe a strategy for using your diagram to find the number that is exactly halfway between these two numbers. Can you think of a mathematical concept or process that this reminds you of? Imagine changing the numbers 0.27 and 0.6 on your magnifier diagram by performing the same operation on both. What happens to the middle number? How does it compare to your original one? Explain your thinking.

TEACHER'S GUIDE

STAGE 1

Problem #1

1. This number line shows one unit. Copy it and label each dot with the correct decimal.

0   1

     a. What happens if you split each of the 10 parts into 10 parts again? What if you continue doing this?
     b. Place a small dot on the line as close as you can to 0.73 units. Explain your thinking.

Questions and Conversations for #1

This section contains ideas for conversations, mainly in the form of questions that students may ask or that you may pose to them. Be sure to allow students to do most of the thinking and talking!

    »   *What are the sizes of each of the parts? How does this relate to place value?* The sizes get one-tenth as large each time you carry out the "splitting" process. Because our place value system uses groups of 10, these sizes will be place values less than one.

Solution for #1

Because the line shows 10 equal parts between 0 and 1, each part has a length of one-tenth, or 0.1 units. You count forward by 0.1 for each dot as you move to the right.

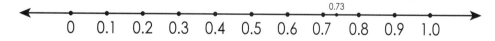

0.73

0   0.1   0.2   0.3   0.4   0.5   0.6   0.7   0.8   0.9   1.0

Solution for a. If each of the 10 parts is split into 10 equal parts, there will be $10 \cdot 10$, or 100 equal parts, and the length of each part will be one-hundredth (0.01) of a unit.

If you continue this process, there will be 10 times as many parts each time: 10, 100, 1000, etc. This means the pattern for the length of the parts is 0.1, 0.01, 0.001, etc. These are getting one-tenth as large each time.

Solution for b. 0.73 is 73 hundredths. Because there are 10 hundredths in 1 tenth, this is also 7 tenths plus 3 hundredths. This means that 0.73 is 3 hundredths of a unit to the right of 0.7, which is a little less than half the distance from 0.7 to 0.8.

Problem #2

2. Explain why 0.7, 0.70, and 0.700 all name the same number.

Questions and Conversations for #2

» *How does it change the way you usually name the number when you place a 0 at the end?* You usually read it using the name of a smallest place value. For example, 0.70 could be read as 70 hundredths instead of 7 tenths.

Solution for #2

0.7 represents 7 tenths. 0.70 stands for 70 hundredths. 0.700 is 700 thousandths. Hundredths are one-tenth as large as tenths, but there are 10 times as many of them, so the numbers are equal. In the same way, because there are 10 times as many thousandths as hundredths, 0.700 is the same number as 0.70.

Problem #3

3. This diagram shows a "number line magnifier"—a magnified view of the interval between two dots on the main number line.

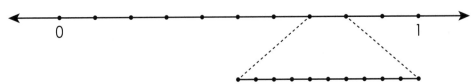

a. Copy the diagram. Label the main number line as "tenths." Then label the magnifier with the appropriate place value name.
b. Mark the numbers 0.73, 0.736 and 0.7368, adding more number line magnifiers as needed. Label each new magnifier with its place value name. Add more digits and more magnifiers if you like!

Teacher's Note. If students are having trouble seeing how to continue the diagram, tell them that each magnifier is attached to the previous one. They should pay close attention to where each magnifier starts and ends.

Solution for #3

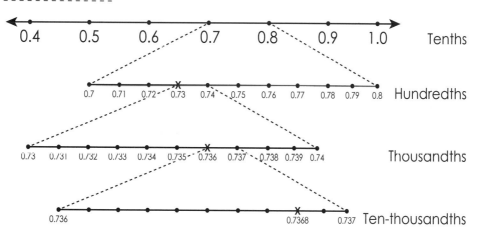

Problem #4

4. You can use place value to name numbers in many ways. For example, some ways to name 473 are:

473 ones   47 tens and 3 ones   4 hundreds, 7 tens, and 3 ones

How could you could name 473 using tenths as one of the place values? Explain your thinking. (There are many possibilities.)

Questions and Conversations for #4

» *How can you generate many solutions that use a single place value name?* Think of what happens every time the value of the place becomes one-tenth as large (or ten times as large).

» *How can you generate many solutions that use multiple place value names?* The possibilities are endless! Choose any digit(s) in the numeral. Then choose any place value name. An example of a creative (even if not very useful) solution would be to rename a number like 2379 as 0.2009 ten-thousands and 3700 tenths.

Teacher's Note. Some students may enjoy taking this process to an extreme. For example, some names for 0.3 are:

3 tenths	30 hundredths
300 thousandths	3000 ten-thousandths
0.3 ones	0.03 tens
0.003 hundreds	0.0003 thousands

Solution for #4

Sample responses: 4730 tenths; 47 tens and 30 tenths; 4 hundreds and 730 tenths; 4 hundreds, 7 tens, and 30 tenths. (Students need only one response.) Because you get tenths by dividing 1 unit into 10 equal parts, there must be 10 times as many tenths as ones.

Problem #5

5. Write at least three ways to use place value to name the number 0.73.

Questions and Conversations for #5

See Questions and Conversations for #4.

Solution for #5

Sample responses: 73 hundredths; 7 tenths and 3 hundredths; 7.3 tenths; 7 tenths and 30 thousandths; 730 thousandths, etc. (Students need three responses.)

Problem #6

6. Write at least five ways to use place value to name the number 0.736.

Questions and Conversations for #6

See Questions and Conversations for #4.

Solution for #6

Sample responses: 736 thousandths; 7 tenths, 3 hundredths, and 6 thousandths; 7 tenths and 36 thousandths; 73 hundredths and 6 thousandths; 7360 ten-thousandths, 7.36 tenths; 73.6 hundredths, etc. (Students need five responses.)

STAGE 2

Problem #7

7. Explain how you can use your diagram from Problem #3 to round 0.7368 to the nearest thousandth, hundredth, tenth, and whole number.

Questions and Conversations for #7

» *What does it mean to round a number?* It means to find the closest number using the specified place value. (You can see the closest number very easily on a number line.)

Solution for #7

The answers are 0.737, 0.74, 0.7, and 1. Rounding a number to a place value means finding the closest number to that place value's level of precision:

0.7368 is closer to 0.737 (than 0.736) on the ten-thousandths magnifier.
0.7368 is closer to 0.74 (than 0.73) on the thousandths magnifier.
0.7368 is closer to 0.7 (than 0.8) on the hundredths magnifier.
0.7368 is closer to 1 (than 0) on the main number line.

Problem #8

8. Explain how you can use your number line diagram to answer these two questions.
   a. Which is greater, 0.7368 or 0.9?
   b. Which is greater, 0.7368 or 0.72?

Questions and Conversations for #8

» *How do you normally use number lines to determine which of two numbers is greater?* The greater number is to the right of the smaller one.

Solution for #8

Solution for a. 0.9 is greater than 0.7368 because 0.9 is to the right of (greater than) every number between 0.7 and 0.8 (see the magnifier) on the number line.

Solution for b. 0.7368 is greater than 0.72 because every number between 0.73 and 0.74 (see the magnifier) is to the right of the number 0.72 on the number line.

Problem #9

9. Draw a number line with two magnifiers to show 0.163. Show how to use your diagram to move 0.702 units to the right of 0.163. Create and solve a real-world story to match this situation.

Questions and Conversations for #9

» *Can it help to rename 0.702?* Possibly. If you think of it as 7 tenths and 2 thousandths instead of 702 thousandths, it might make it easier to count your way forward.

» *What operation is involved?* Addition.

» *What kinds of real-world things are measured to the thousandths place?* Consider looking for examples from sports or science.

> **Teacher's Note.** Challenge students to make their real-world examples as realistic as possible for the size and precision of the numbers. Encourage them to look for ideas online. This can help them develop a sense for the sizes of real-world quantities.

Solution for #9

There are two magnifiers on the left showing 0.163.
Slide the magnifiers 7 tenths of a unit to the right. (See the upper arrow.)
Slide the small x 2 thousandths of a unit to the right. (See the lower arrow.)

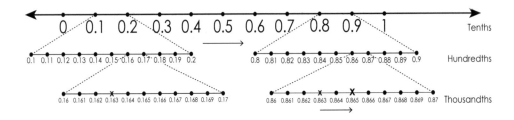

Sample story: Danica and Jolene have set a goal to make the combined time they are short of a swimming record less than 0.9 seconds. At the most recent meet, Danica missed the record by 0.163 seconds and Jolene missed it by 0.702 seconds. Did they achieve their goal?

Answer: Yes, because $0.163 + 0.702 = 0.865$ and 0.865 seconds is less than 0.9 seconds.

Problem #10

10. Draw a magnifier diagram that shows 0.9 and 0.58. Explain how to use your diagram to show how far apart these numbers are. Create and solve a real-world story to match this situation.

Questions and Conversations for #10

» *How would a "counting up" strategy look on a number line with a magnifier?* Try doing it in steps, once on the magnifier, and once on the main number line.

» *What operation tells you how far apart two numbers are?* Subtraction.

Solution for #10

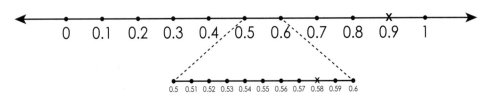

Sample response: Start at 0.58 and count up 2 hundredths to 0.6. Then count up 3 tenths to 0.9. All together, you have counted up 3 tenths and 2 hundredths, so 0.58 and 0.9 are 32 hundredths (0.32) of a unit apart.

Sample story: A cup of grapes has 0.58 grams of protein, while a cup of bananas has 0.9 grams. Which has more protein, and how much more?

Answer: A cup of bananas has 0.32 grams more protein than a cup of grapes. The number line shows that 0.9 is greater than 0.58 by an amount 0.32. We could also write a number model for this:

$$0.9 - 0.58 = 0.32$$

Problem #11

11. Why might it be harder to create a realistic story using the numbers 0.9 and 0.58114 (instead of 0.9 and 0.58)?

Teacher's Note. It's not necessarily clear how precisely the 0.9 was measured in our story. If it were measured to the nearest hundredth, it would have been better to write it as 0.90. If it were measured only to the nearest tenth, it might have been better to round the answer to 0.3.

Questions and Conversations for #11

» *What is the most obvious difference between the numbers?* One number was measured much more precisely than the other.

Solution for #11

It's harder to create a realistic subtraction story for 0.9 and 0.58114 because they have such different levels of precision. It's not likely that the same quantity would be measured to the nearest tenth or hundredth in one case, and to the nearest hundred-thousandth in the other.

STAGE 3

Problem #12

12. Draw a number line magnifier diagram that shows 0.27 and 0.6. Describe a strategy for using your diagram to find the number that is exactly halfway between these two numbers. Can you think of a mathematical concept or process that this reminds you of? Imagine changing the numbers 0.27 and 0.6 on your magnifier diagram by performing the same operation on both. What happens to the middle number? How does it compare to your original one? Explain your thinking.

Questions and Conversations for #12

» *Does it matter what operation you use to change the numbers?* In many cases, it won't matter. For example, you could multiply 0.27 and 0.6 by the same (positive) number. Multiplying them by 10 might be an interesting thing to try. You could also consider adding the same number to both. (Can you think of operations that would cause problems? What would go wrong?)

Solution for #12

It's not very practical to draw magnifiers for everything between 0.27 and 0.6. But you can still use the diagram to help you visualize what it would look like.

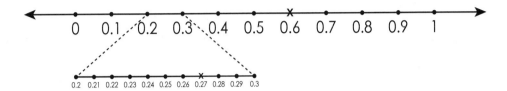

Sample student response 1: Move in toward the center by the same amount on the left and right.

Move	Left	Right
move in 1 tenth	0.37 (slide the magnifier)	0.5
move in 3 hundredths	0.4	0.47
move in 3 hundredths	0.43	0.44

The middle number must be halfway between these, which is 0.435.

Sample student response 2: Count the distance between 0.27 and 0.6 as 0.33 units. Think of this as 330 thousandths and take half of it to get 165 thousandths. Count forward from 0.27 by 1 tenth (0.37), then 6 hundredths (0.43), and then 5 thousandths (0.435).

Sample student response 3: This strategy is a little harder to visualize on the number line, but some students may take half of each number and then add the results. Half of 270 thousandths is 135 thousandths. Adding 3 tenths to this, we get $0.135 + 0.3 = 0.435$.

The number that is exactly in the middle of any two numbers on the number line is just the average of the two numbers. If some students noticed this earlier, their strategy for finding the middle number may have been to add the numbers and divide by 2!

Sample student response for the final task: Suppose you multiply both numbers by 10. This would make every label on the number line ten times larger. 0.27 would become 2.7 and 0.6 would become 6. The middle number would now be 4.35, which is also 10 times as large as 0.435.

Teacher's Note. Some students might be interested in exploring what goes wrong if you multiply both numbers by a negative number, or if you square them.

WRAP UP

Share Strategies

Have students share their strategies and ideas.

Discuss students' stories. Are they realistic? How do they connect to the meanings of addition and subtraction? How well do the real-life quantities that the students chose match the size and precision of the numbers they were given? (It can often be surprisingly difficult to make this happen!)

Summarize

Answer any remaining questions that students have. Summarize key points:

» If comparing, rounding, adding, or subtracting decimals are relatively new ideas to students, have them discuss their strategies using the magnifiers. Then ask them how they could accomplish the same things without the magnifiers—just by looking at the numerals.

» If students already know procedures for comparing, rounding, adding, or subtracting decimals, ask them to use the magnifier diagrams to explain why the procedures work.

Further Exploration

Ask students to think of ways to continue or extend this exploration. Here are some possibilities:

» Make number lines with physical magnifiers that you can actually slide. Practice using them to compare, round, add, and subtract decimals, including numbers less than one ten-thousandth. (*Teacher's Note*: You could use plastic sheet protectors or lamination so that students can mark and erase labels for points on their lines.)

» Do some research and create stories involving quantities you don't know much about. For example, you could use units from science such as voltage, luminosity, force, pressure, density, momentum, charge, angular velocity, or frequency.

» Find ways to use number lines and magnifiers to help visualize multiplication and division. Create stories based on these operations.

Exploration 4

Million, Billion, Trillion . . .

INTRODUCTION

Materials

- » Scientific calculator

Prior Knowledge

- » Know place values from one through one trillion.
- » Understand that the value of each place is related to the next by a factor of 10.
- » Understand the meaning of exponents.

Learning Goals

- » Improve number sense for large numbers.
- » Understand the role of place value when multiplying powers of 10.
- » Solve problems involving multiplication and division of large numbers.
- » Reason about size relationships between large numbers.
- » Explore scientific notation: why it is used, how to represent it on a calculator, and how to apply it to solve problems.
- » Communicate complex mathematical ideas clearly.
- » Persist in solving challenging problems.

> **Teacher's Note.** Students do not have to know procedures for multiplying by powers of 10 or writing numbers in scientific notation. You could use this activity to begin exploring these concepts with them.

Launching the Exploration

Motivation and purpose. To students: Million, billion, trillion . . . The words look and sound almost the same! Are the numbers nearly the same, too? You'll find out how they compare when you explore large number place values in this activity.

Understanding the problem. Discuss the meaning of *standard notation* (the usual way of writing a number). In Stage 2, students are introduced to *number-word notation* and *scientific notation*, which will be described at that time.

Show students how to use the exponent key on their calculator. This usually looks like $\wedge$, y^x, or x^y.

Look through the entire exploration (or the part that students will be doing) to get a sense for the big picture. Stage 1 is about exploring relationships among powers of 10. In Stage 2, the focus is on *scientific notation*. And in Stage 3, students apply their new knowledge to investigate the effects of doubling.

Students may use a scientific calculator for Problems #3, #4, #7, #8, and #9. "Showing work" means documenting the calculations they did along with the results (including units). It doesn't necessarily mean showing details of algorithms such as long division.

STUDENT HANDOUT

Stage 1

Because our place value system is based on groups of 10, we can use powers of 10 to help us read, write, and calculate numbers.

1. Copy, continue, and complete the table for place values from one through one trillion. Explain your answer for the entries in the "ones" row.

Place Value	Distance From Ones Place	Power of 10	Standard Notation
ones	0		
tens	1	10^1	
hundreds	2		
thousands	3		1000

2. Answer the questions. Then use standard notation to write a multiplication or division sentence for each. Rewrite each equation using exponential expressions with bases of ten.
    a. How many thousands are in one million?

    b. How many ten thousands are in one million?

    c. How many millions are in one billion?

    d. How many billions are in one trillion?

    e. How many millions are in one trillion?

    f. Describe any patterns you see in the equations with the exponential expressions.

For Problems #3 and #4, show your work, including units. Explain your strategies.
3. Answer these questions:
    a. How old will you be 1 million seconds from now?

    b. How old will you be 1 billion seconds from now?

    c. How old will you be 1 trillion seconds from now?

4. Answer these questions:
    a. If you were 1 million inches from where you are now, where might you be?

    b. If you were 1 billion inches from where you are now, where might you be?

    c. If you were 1 trillion inches from where you are now, where might you be?

Advanced Common Core Math Explorations: Numbers & Operations © Prufrock Press Inc.

Exploration 4: Million, Billion, Trillion . . .

d. If you were 1 million centimeters from where you are now, where might you be? (Try using mental math for this one!)

e. Why is it easier to use mental math when the units are centimeters?

Stage 2

5. Use number-word notation to name each number in at least five ways.
   a. 78,000

   b. 692,000

   c. 10,000,000

6. Complete a table like the one above to show these numbers in scientific notation:
   a. 7,000,000,000

   b. 350,900,000

   c. 58,100,000,000,000

   d. 4.9

7. Multiply $5 \cdot 5 \cdot 5 \cdot 5 \cdot 5 \ldots$ etc., on a scientific calculator.
   a. Keep going until your calculator automatically shifts into scientific notation. How many factors of five did you have to multiply to make this happen? Why do you think the notation changed?

   b. Show an example of what a number in scientific notation looks like on your calculator's display. Write the number in standard notation as well.

Stage 3

8. If you fold a piece of paper once, it will be 2 pages thick. If you fold it twice, it will be 4 pages thick. How many folds will it take for it to become more than 1000 pages thick? 1 million? 1 billion? 1 trillion? 1 quadrillion (10^{15})? Describe any patterns that you notice. Explain what causes them.

9. A package of 500 sheets of paper is 2 inches thick. How tall will the stack be if you fold one sheet of this paper 42 times? Just for fun, make a guess before you begin!

10. Find an algebraic expression that will calculate the thickness (number of sheets) if you fold a page k times. What happens if $k = 0$?

11. Which is larger, $\left(10^{10}\right)^{10}$ or $10^{\left(10^{10}\right)}$—or are they equal? Explain.

TEACHER'S GUIDE

STAGE 1

Problem #1

Because our place value system is based on groups of 10, we can use powers of 10 to help us read, write, and calculate numbers.

1. Copy, continue, and complete the table for place values from one through one trillion. Explain your answer for the entries in the "ones" row.

Place Value	Distance From Ones Place	Power of 10	Standard Notation
ones	0		
tens	1	10^1	
hundreds	2		
thousands	3		1000

Questions and Conversations for #1

This section contains ideas for conversations, mainly in the form of questions that students may ask or that you may pose to them. Be sure to allow students to do most of the thinking and talking!

» *What happens to the value of the digit 1 each time you move it one place to the left?* When it moves one place to the left, its value becomes 10 times greater.

» *Does this idea apply to numbers with more than one digit?* Yes. For example, look at the number 24. If you shift the 2 and the 4 from the tens and ones to the hundreds and tens places, each value becomes 10 times greater ($20 \cdot 10 = 200$ and $4 \cdot 10 = 40$), and therefore, so does the entire number.

> *Teacher's Note for #1.* We focus on the values of the digits instead of "counting zeros" in order to keep students' attention on place value and the sizes of the numbers.

Solution for #1

Place Value	Distance From Ones Place	Power of 10	Standard Notation
ones	0	10^0	1
tens	1	10^1	10
hundreds	2	10^2	100
thousands	3	10^3	1000
ten-thousands	4	10^4	10,000
hundred-thousands	5	10^5	100,000
millions	6	10^6	1,000,000
ten-millions	7	10^7	10,000,000
hundred-millions	8	10^8	100,000,000
billions	9	10^9	1,000,000,000
ten-billions	10	10^{10}	10,000,000,000
hundred-billions	11	10^{11}	100,000,000,000
trillions	12	10^{12}	1,000,000,000,000

The exponent on the power of 10 is the same as the distance from the ones place. Because the ones place is a distance of 0 from itself, its power of 10 is 10^0, and $10^0 = 1$. Notice that each time the exponent decreases by 1, the value divides by 10.

Problem #2

2. Answer the questions. Then use standard notation to write a multiplication or division sentence for each. Rewrite each equation using exponential expressions with bases of ten.
   a. How many thousands are in one million?
   b. How many ten thousands are in one million?
   c. How many millions are in one billion?
   d. How many billions are in one trillion?
   e. How many millions are in one trillion?
   f. Describe any patterns you see in the equations with the exponential expressions.

Questions and Conversations for #2

» *How far does the digit 1 move between 1000 and 1,000,000? What does this tell you about the relative sizes of the numbers?* It moves three places, which makes one million 1000 times larger than 1000.

Solution for #2

Solution for a. There are 1000 thousands in one million.

$$1000 \times 1000 = 1,000,000$$
$$10^3 \times 10^3 = 10^6 \text{, or}$$
$$1,000,000 \div 1000 = 1000$$
$$10^6 \div 10^3 = 10^3$$

Solution for b. There are 100 ten-thousands in one million.

$$100 \times 10,000 = 1,000,000$$
$$10^2 \times 10^4 = 10^6 \text{, or}$$
$$1,000,000 \div 10,000 = 100$$
$$10^6 \div 10^4 = 10^2$$

> **Teacher's Note for #2.** If students are writing out long division or multiplication calculations with many zeros, suggest that they look for more efficient methods. If they are "crossing off zeros" to divide, encourage them to think about what happens to the sizes of the numbers each time they cross off a zero. (They get one tenth as large.)

Solution for c. There are 1000 millions in one billion.

$$1000 \times 1,000,000 = 1,000,000,000 \qquad 10^3 \times 10^6 = 10^9 \text{, or}$$
$$1,000,000,000 \div 1,000,000 = 1000 \qquad 10^9 \div 10^6 = 10^3$$

Solution for d. There are 1000 billions in one trillion.

$$1000 \times 1,000,000,000 = 1,000,000,000,000 \qquad 10^3 \times 10^9 = 10^{12} \text{, or}$$
$$1,000,000,000,000 \div 1,000,000,000 = 1000 \qquad 10^{12} \div 10^9 = 10^3$$

Solution for e. There are 1,000,000 millions in one trillion.

$$1,000,000 \times 1,000,000 = 1,000,000,000,000 \qquad 10^6 \times 10^6 = 10^{12} \text{, or}$$
$$1,000,000,000,000 \div 1,000,000 = 1,000,000 \qquad 10^{12} \div 10^6 = 10^6$$

Solution for f. The sum of the exponents in the factors equals the exponent in the product. (For the division sentences, the exponents subtract instead.) This makes sense because each exponent tracks the location or movement of the digit 1. For example, in the change from 10,000 (10^4) to 1,000,000 (10^6), the 1 begins 4 places to the left of the ones, shifts 2 more places, and ends up 6 places to the left of the ones.

Problem #3

For Problems #3 and #4, show your work, including units. Explain your strategies.

    3. Answer these questions:

        a. How old will you be 1 million seconds from now?

        b. How old will you be 1 billion seconds from now?

        c. How old will you be 1 trillion seconds from now?

Questions and Conversations for #3

    » *What units should you use in your answers?* Answer the questions using units that will be easy to understand and visualize.

    » *Should you round your answers?* Probably. You are just trying to get a sense for the size of the numbers, so answers with many decimal places are probably more distracting than helpful.

    » *What can you do if a number (say one trillion) is too big to enter into your calculator?* Get creative! Think about ways to enter it without typing in each digit.

    » *Can you use your answers for one million seconds or inches to help you find the answers for one billion and one trillion?* Yes. Think about how one billion compares with one million.

Solution for #3

Solution for a. You will be about a week and a half older!

$$1{,}000{,}000 \text{ sec} \div 60 \text{ sec per min} \approx 16{,}667 \text{ min}$$

$$16{,}667 \text{ min} \div 60 \text{ min per hr} \approx 278 \text{ hr}$$

$$278 \text{ hr} \div 24 \text{ hr per day} \approx 11.6 \text{ days}$$

Solution for b. Because 1 billion is 1000 millions, you would be about $11.6 \cdot 1000 = 11{,}600$ days older. Now, 11,600 days $\div$ 365 days per year $\approx$ 32 years, so you would be about 32 years older than you are now. Middle school students will be in their early to mid-40s!

Solution for c. Because 1 trillion is 1000 billions, you would be about $32 \cdot 1000 = 32{,}000$ years old!

Problem #4

    4. Answer these questions:

        a. If you were 1 million inches from where you are now, where might you be?

        b. If you were 1 billion inches from where you are now, where might you be?

    c. If you were 1 trillion inches from where you are now, where might you be?

    d. If you were 1 million centimeters from where you are now, where might you be? (Try using mental math for this one!)

    e. Why is it easier to use mental math when the units are centimeters?

Questions and Conversations for #4

See Questions and Conversations for #3.

Solution for #4

Solution for a. You might be in a nearby town—about 16 miles from you.

$$1,000,000 \text{ in} \div 12 \text{ in per ft} \approx 83,333 \text{ ft}$$

$$83,333 \text{ ft} \div 5280 \text{ ft per mi} \approx 16 \text{ mi}$$

Solution for b. Because 1 billion is 1000 millions, you would be about $16 \cdot 1000 = 16,000$ miles away—more than halfway around the world!

Solution for c. Because 1 trillion is 1000 billions, you would be about $16,000 \cdot 1000 = 16,000,000$ miles from where you are now. This would be far out in space—about $\frac{2}{3}$ of the way to the orbit of Venus!

Solution for d. 1 cm is 0.01 meters. To find 1,000,000 of these, shift the 1 six places to the left to get 10,000 meters. 1000 meters is 1 kilometer, so 10,000 meters is 10 kilometers.

People who grew up using the metric system probably have a good feel for how long 10 kilometers is. For those who didn't, it helps to know that 1 kilometer is about 0.6 miles, so 10 kilometers is close to 6 miles.

It is usually easier to calculate with metric measurements because they are based on powers of 10, just like our place value system.

STAGE 2

Problem #5

You can use place value to name numbers in many ways. For example, you may write 1300 as: 1 thousand and 3 hundreds; 13 hundreds; 130 tens; 1 thousand and 30 tens; 1.3 thousands; 0.13 ten-thousands, etc. These are all forms of *number-word notation*.

Teacher's Note. Stage 2 isn't necessarily meant as a complete lesson on scientific notation. It introduces students to the concept using the idea of *order of magnitude*. This is to direct their attention to the place value instead of just "moving the decimal."

Teacher's Note. Continued.

Students should know that people don't always use the term *order of magnitude* in a precise or consistent way. For example, using our approach, the number 98 has an order of magnitude of "tens" because that is its highest place value. On the other hand, some would say that its order of magnitude is "hundreds" because it is clearly nearer to 100 than 10. Also, you can name the order of magnitude using the exponent on the power of 10 instead of the place value (i.e., "2" instead of "hundreds"). I have chosen the approach in this book in order to help students make clear connections between scientific notation and place value. The key idea is that an order of magnitude is essentially a power of 10.

5. Use number-word notation to name each number in at least five ways.
   a. 78,000
   b. 692,000
   c. 10,000,000

Solution for #5

Sample student responses (students need only five answers for each):

Responses for a: 7 ten thousands and 8 thousands; 7.8 ten-thousands; 780 hundreds; 7 ten thousands and 80 hundreds; 7800 tens; 78,000 ones; 70 thousands and 80 hundreds

Responses for b: 6 hundred-thousands, 9 ten-thousands, and 2 thousands; 690 thousands and 20 hundreds; 6.92 hundred-thousands; 6 hundred-thousands and 92 thousands; 692 thousands; 60 ten-thousands, 90 thousands, and 20 hundreds

Responses for c: 0.01 billions; 1 ten-millions; 10 millions; 100 hundred-thousands; 1000 ten-thousands; 10,000 thousands; 100,000 hundreds; 1,000,000 tens; 10,000,000 ones; 1,000,000,000 hundredths

Teacher's Note. Some students may be very creative. For example, in part (a), 78,000 might be written 6 ten-thousands, 10 thousands, 7 thousands, and 10 hundreds. This is certainly not traditional number-word notation! However, the precise form of the answer is not what is important here. What is important is that students' answers have the correct value. Creative answers like this can lead to excellent conversation and learning opportunities.

Problem #6

A very helpful way to write a large number is to name it using its highest place value—also known as its *order of magnitude*. When you express the order of magnitude as a power of 10, you are writing the number in *scientific notation*. Study the examples on the next page.

Standard Notation	Order of Magnitude Notation	Scientific Notation
40,000,000,000	4 ten-billions	4×10^{10}
9,500,000	9.5 millions	9.5×10^6
677,000,000,000,000	6.77 hundred-trillions	6.77×10^{14}

6. Complete a table like the one above to show these numbers in scientific notation:
   a. 7,000,000,000
   b. 350,900,000
   c. 58,100,000,000,000
   d. 4.9

Questions and Conversations for #6

» *What are the advantages of writing large numbers in scientific notation?* They can be easier to read, write, and calculate in this form. It is very easy to get a quick read on the size of a number in scientific notation because its power of 10 is the same as its order of magnitude (its approximate size based on place value).

» *Why does the first part of the number in scientific notation always have an order of magnitude of ones?* This happens automatically when the power of 10 equals the order of magnitude of the original number.

Solution for #6

Standard Notation	Order of Magnitude Notation	Scientific Notation
7,000,000,000	7 billions	7×10^9
350,900,000	3.509 hundred-millions	3.509×10^8
58,100,000,000,000	5.81 ten-trillions	5.81×10^{13}
4.9	4.9 ones	4.9×10^0

Problem #7

7. Multiply $5 \cdot 5 \cdot 5 \cdot 5 \cdot 5 \ldots$ etc., on a scientific calculator.
   a. Keep going until your calculator automatically shifts into scientific notation. How many

Teacher's Note. Of course, it looks strange to write 4.9 in scientific notation! This is included mainly to keep connecting the idea of an exponent of 0 with the number 1.

factors of five did you have to multiply to make this happen? Why do you think the notation changed?

b. Show an example of what a number in scientific notation looks like on your calculator's display. Write the number in standard notation as well.

Teacher's Note. After students have completed Problem #7, ask them to experiment with their calculators, predicting and testing what happens when they multiply numbers in scientific notation by simple numbers such as 2, 5, or 10. For example:

- What happens when you multiply 6.4×10^{14} by 10? Why? (Answer: 6.4×10^{15})
- What happens when you multiply 6.4×10^{14} by 2? Why? (Answer: 1.28×10^{15})

Solution for #7

Solution for a. Many students' calculators will probably shift into scientific notation after multiplying between 10–15 factors of five. This happens when the numeral has too many digits to fit in the display.

Solution for b. Scientific notation is shown differently on different calculators. For example, the number 28,000,000,000,000 might look like any of these expressions:

$$2.8 \times 10^{13} \qquad 2.8_{\times 10}13$$

$$2.8 \ 13 \qquad 2.8e13$$

STAGE 3

Problem #8

8. If you fold a piece of paper once, it will be 2 pages thick. If you fold it twice, it will be 4 pages thick. How many folds will it take for it to become more than 1000 pages thick? 1 million? 1 billion? 1 trillion? 1 quadrillion $\left(10^{15}\right)$? Describe any patterns that you notice. Explain what causes them.

Questions and Conversations for #8

» *Is it possible actually to do these folds?* No. Students may experiment to see that about 7 folds is the most they can do.

» *What happens to the thickness each time you make another fold?* It doubles.

» *After you find the answer for 1 thousand, can you predict the answer for 1 million?* Yes, you can. Try thinking this through before you calculate!

» *Will the pattern of 10, 20, 30, 40, and 50 folds continue forever?* No, because 2^{10} is a little bit greater than 1000.

Teacher's Note. If students' calculators display a number like 2×10^{14} as "2. 14" or "2e14," caution them not to confuse this with 2^{14}!

Solution for #8

The number of sheets follows the doubling pattern

$$2, 4, 8, 16, 32, 64, 128, 256, 512, 1024 \ldots$$

You pass 1000 on the 10th fold (1024 sheets).

Because the number of sheets doubles each time you make a fold, the process involves powers of 2.

$$1 \text{ fold:} \quad 2^1 = 2 \text{ sheets}$$

$$2 \text{ folds:} \quad 2^2 = 4 \text{ sheets}$$

$$3 \text{ folds:} \quad 2^3 = 8 \text{ sheets, etc.}$$

This shows that the exponent equals the number of folds, so we get:

$$10 \text{ folds:} \quad 2^{10} = 1024 \text{ sheets}$$

$$20 \text{ folds:} \quad 2^{20} = 1,048,576 \text{ sheets}$$

$$30 \text{ folds:} \quad 2^{30} = 1,073,741,824 \text{ sheets}$$

$$40 \text{ folds:} \quad 2^{40} \approx 1.0995 \times 10^{12} \text{ sheets}$$

$$50 \text{ folds:} \quad 2^{50} \approx 1.1259 \times 10^{15} \text{ sheets}$$

You pass the thousand, million, billion, trillion, and quadrillion marks when the number of folds is 10, 20, 30, 40, and 50 respectively.

This pattern occurs because 2^{10} is a little larger than 1000. Each time you fold another 10 times, you are multiplying again by a number just larger than 1000. This gives results just larger than 1 million, 1 billion, 1 trillion, etc.

Problem #9

9. A package of 500 sheets of paper is 2 inches thick. How tall will the stack be if you fold one sheet of this paper 42 times? Just for fun, make a guess before you begin!

Questions and Conversations for #9

» *What do you think are the best units to use in your answer? Why?* As before, choose units that will be easy to understand and visualize.

Solution for #9

The stack will be about 278,000 miles tall!

Each sheet of paper is $2 \div 500 = .004$ inches thick. You need to double this 42 times:

$$0.004 \times 2^{42} \approx 0.004 \times \left(4.398 \times 10^{12}\right) \approx 1.76 \times 10^{10} \text{ inches}$$

or about 17.6 billion inches. To make this easier to understand, you can rewrite it in terms of miles:

$$\left(1.76 \times 10^{10}\right) \text{ in} \div 12 \text{ in per ft} \div 5280 \text{ ft per mile} \approx 278{,}000 \text{ miles}.$$

For perspective, the moon is about 240,000 miles from the Earth!

Problem #10

10. Find an algebraic expression that will calculate the thickness (number of sheets) if you fold a page k times. What happens if $k = 0$?

Solution for #10

We calculate the number of sheets by taking 2 to the power of the number of folds. Therefore, for k folds, the algebraic expression for the number of sheets is 2^k.

For 0 folds, there is 1 sheet. This suggests that $2^0 = 1$, the same answer we found for 10^0 in Problem #1 when we were using place value to explore exponents.

Problem #11

11. Which is larger, $\left(10^{10}\right)^{10}$ or $10^{\left(10^{10}\right)}$—or are they equal? Explain.

Teacher's Notes. To get a feel for this, imagine trying to write these two numerals down. Although a googol is an incredibly large number—much larger than anything we normally need—it would only take a minute or two to write it down, because its numeral has "only" one hundred zeros.

The numeral for $10^{10{,}000{,}000{,}000}$ has 10 billion zeros. If we wrote a digit each second, it would take 10 billion seconds to write. We learned in Problem #3 that 1 billion seconds is about 32 years, so 10 billion seconds is about 320 years—and this is just the time it would take to write it down! It doesn't capture the full sense of the size of the actual number. After all, at this rate, it would only take 7 seconds to write the number 1,000,000—even though it is obviously a very large number!

Questions and Conversations for #11

» *How far does the digit 1 move in each case?*

Solution for #11

$\left(10^{10}\right)^{10} = (10{,}000{,}000{,}000)^{10} = 10^{100}$. 10 billion to the 10th power is 10^{100} because, beginning from the ones place, the digit 1 shifts 10 places to the left, 10 times—a total shift of 100 places. The resulting numeral looks a 1 followed by 100 zeros. This number is called a *googol*.

$10^{\left(10^{10}\right)} = 10^{10{,}000{,}000{,}000}$. Because this is 10 billion one-digit shifts, its numeral looks like 1 followed by 10 billion zeros! This number is vastly larger than a googol!

WRAP UP

Share Strategies

Have students share their strategies and compare results.

Summarize

Answer any remaining questions that students have. Summarize key points:

» Because every place value is 10 times greater than the one to the right of it, you can express place values in exponential form as powers of 10.

» Procedures for multiplying and dividing by powers of 10 that involve "adding zeros," "crossing off zeros," and "moving the decimal" all work by shifting the place values of the digits.

» Scientific notation is most often used for working with very large (and very small) numbers. The power of 10 gives a quick read on the overall size of the number.

» You have seen one or two examples of cases in which a base with an exponent of 0 has a value of 1.

» You can use properties of exponents to represent and apply patterns in calculations that involve powers of 10.

Further Exploration

Ask students to think of ways to continue or extend this exploration. Here are some possibilities:

» Investigate other ideas for visualizing large numbers. For example, how many books (or libraries) would a million, billion, or trillion letters or words fill? How much space would a million, billion, or trillion "small" place value blocks fill? What would a million blades of grass look like? What might weigh a million pounds? About how many breaths will you take or how many times will your heart beat in your lifetime? Create and explore your own ideas.

» Watch the classic short film, *Powers of Ten* (http://www.powersof10.com/film).

» The phrase *order of magnitude* is especially useful for describing comparisons or changes in large quantities. Read about how scientists and others use this term.

» Look up the story behind the words *googol* and *googolplex*.

» Do some research on names and metric prefixes of very large numbers.

Exploration 5

Discovering Divisibility Tests

Materials

» Graph paper (for drawing diagrams of Base Ten blocks)

Prior Knowledge

» Be familiar with Base Ten blocks—cubes or smalls (ones), longs (tens), and flats (hundreds).
» Understand what it means for one number to be divisible by another.

Learning Goals

» Use place value flexibly to represent numbers.
» Use conceptual understanding of place value to justify and create divisibility tests.
» Make connections between different representations of place value.
» Reason abstractly with place value concepts.
» Increase fluency with testing numbers for divisibility.
» Communicate complex mathematical ideas clearly.
» Persist in solving challenging problems.

Launching the Exploration

Motivation and purpose. To students: You know that a number is divisible by 5 if the ones digit is 0 or 5. You may even know how to test for divisibility by 3 by adding a number's digits. Divisibility tests like these allow us to determine if one number is divisible by another without actually doing the division. There are many of these tests and they are all based on place value concepts. In this exploration, you will have an opportunity to explore some of these connections and to use what you learn to create your own divisibility tests!

Understanding the problem. Have students share what they already know about divisibility tests.

Look through the entire activity with students to help them see the big picture. At the beginning, they use Base Ten blocks to justify well-known divisibility tests. Later,

71

they examine tests that are more challenging to understand. Finally, they use what they have learned to develop their own tests.

As students begin work, have them use graph paper for their drawings, with each square representing a single cube. Check that they understand the ideas well enough to work independently.

STUDENT HANDOUT

Stage 1

1. A number is divisible by 4 if its final two digits form a number that is divisible by 4. Create a drawing of Base Ten blocks to represent the number 136. Use your drawing to explain why the divisibility test works.

2. A number is divisible by 3 if the sum of its digits is divisible by 3.
    a. Create a drawing of Base Ten blocks to represent the number 72. Show what happens if you remove one block from each of the longs (tens) and move these blocks over with the smalls (ones).

    b. Use your drawing(s) to explain why the divisibility test for 3 works. What happens with numbers that have three or more digits?

3. Use your experience with the divisibility test for 3 to create and justify a test for divisibility by 9. Use an example. What do the tests have in common? Why will this idea work only for 3 and 9?

4. Now you will create a divisibility test for 11.
    a. Show the number 143 using only longs and smalls—no flats. Use as many longs as possible. Show what happens if you join as many smalls as possible to a long. How can you see at a glance that 143 is divisible by 11?

    b. Create a test for divisibility by 11. Explain your thinking.

    c. How and why will your test work with four-digit numbers?

Stage 2

5. Choose one or both of the approaches in parts a and b to create a divisibility test for 7. Use the number 154 to illustrate your thinking process.
   a. Transfer some smalls to or from each long.

   b. Double the number that you're testing by doubling the number of longs and smalls. Then group the longs into pairs and join a small to as many pairs as possible.

   c. These two methods lead to different tests. Tell which test you prefer and why.

Stage 3

6. Create a divisibility test for 13. Explain your thinking process and justify the procedure.

7. Describe a general procedure for creating divisibility tests. Explain how to use it to find a test for 17. For what types of numbers can you create a test like this?

8. There is a test for divisibility by 11 that is especially helpful for large numbers. Use these tables to help you develop this test. Explain your thinking and justify your procedure based on patterns in these tables.

	Divided by 11			Divided by 11
9	$0.\overline{81}$		11	1
99	9		101	$9.\overline{18}$
999	$90.\overline{81}$		1001	91
9999	909		10,001	$909.\overline{18}$
99,999	$9090.\overline{81}$		100,001	9091
999,999	90,909		1,000,001	$90,909.\overline{18}$
9,999,999	$909,090.\overline{81}$		10,000,001	909,091

Note. There are many fascinating patterns to explore here. For now, focus on the parts that can help you create the divisibility test.

TEACHER'S GUIDE

STAGE 1

Problem #1

1. A number is divisible by 4 if its final two digits form a number that is divisible by 4. Create a drawing of Base Ten blocks to represent the number 136. Use your drawing to explain why the divisibility test works.

Questions and Conversations for #1

This section contains ideas for conversations, mainly in the form of questions that students may ask or that you may pose to them. Be sure to allow students to do most of the thinking and talking!

» *How can you use your drawing to show that 136 is divisible by 4?* One possibility is to decompose it into groups of four.

» *Why might it be best to decompose the flat before the longs and smalls?* This is easier because the flat can be split into a whole number of groups of four.

» *Why can you focus just on the tens and ones (the longs and smalls) to determine divisibility by 4?* No matter how many flats there are, they will always contain a whole number of groups of four.

Solution for #1

This picture shows that 136 is divisible by four because it can be split into a whole number of groups of four.

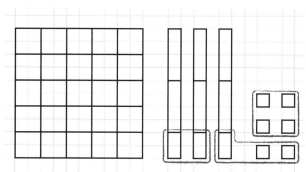

Every flat (group of 100) will always contain 25 groups of four, so you only have to look at the longs (tens) and smalls (ones) to see if they contain a whole number of groups of four. These are represented by the final two digits.

Problem #2

2. A number is divisible by 3 if the sum of its digits is divisible by 3.
   a. Create a drawing of Base Ten blocks to represent the number 72. Show what happens if you remove one block from each of the longs (tens) and move these blocks over with the smalls (ones).
   b. Use your drawing(s) to explain why the divisibility test for 3 works. What happens with numbers that have three or more digits?

Questions and Conversations for #2

» *Why do you remove a block from each of the longs?* It creates groups of nine, each of which is 3 groups of three.

» *Why don't you have to look at the longs after one small is removed from each?* You already know that they contain a whole number of groups of three.

» *How can you predict, just by looking at the numeral 72, how many smalls (ones) there will be after transferring the cubes from the longs to the smalls? Why?* You can just add the digits $(7 + 2)$, because you will have one small from each of the 7 longs plus the original 2 smalls.

» *For numerals with more than two digits, how many cubes should you remove from larger place value groups such as hundreds, thousands, etc.? Why?* You should still remove one cube from each because when you subtract 1 from a power of 10, the result (99, 999, etc.) will always be divisible by 3.

Solution for #2

Solution for a. If you move one block from each long in the first picture over to the smalls (grey blocks in the second picture), the longs become groups of nine (3 groups of three) so that you can focus just on the smalls (ones)! If they have a whole number of groups of three, then so does the original number.

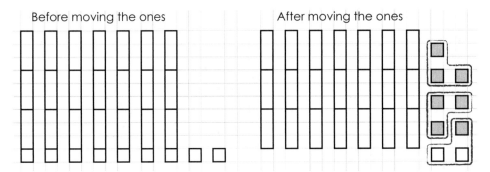

In this picture, there are $2 + 7 = 9$ ones—the 2 we started with plus one from each of the 7 longs. We can see this just by adding the digits of 72! Because this sum is divisible by 3, so is 72.

Solution for b. What if you have a number with three or more digits?

Sample student response 1: I will use an example to explain: You can decompose 3724 into 372 longs and 4 smalls. After you move one small from each long to the ones, you will have $372 + 4 = 376$ ones.

Now you can use the test again! 376 has 37 longs and 6 smalls. Assuming you move one small from each of these longs, you will have $37 + 6 = 43$ smalls. Because 43 isn't divisible by 3, neither is 376, and so neither is 3724!

Sample student response 2: I took one away from every place value group (except the ones) and moved it to the ones. The 1000s became 999s. The 100s became 99s, etc. All of these groups are divisible by 3, so I could just look at the ones.

For example, with the number 3724:

3 thousands → 3 groups of 999
7 hundreds → 7 groups of 99
2 tens → 2 groups of 9
4 ones → $3 + 7 + 2 + 4$ ones

Because $3 + 7 + 2 + 4 = 16$ is not divisible by 3, neither is 3724.

Problem #3

3. Use your experience with the divisibility test for 3 to create and justify a test for divisibility by 9. Use an example. What do the tests have in common? Why will this idea work only for 3 and 9?

Solution for #3

You can still remove one small from each place value group, because $9, 99, 999$, etc., are divisible by 9 as well as three! The only difference is that the sum of the digits must be divisible by 9 instead of 3. For example, 567 is divisible by 9 because $5 + 6 + 7 = 18$, which is divisible by 9.

This type of test (sums of digits) won't work for other numbers because 3 and 9 are the only whole numbers except 1 that always divide evenly into $9, 99, 999$, etc.

Problem #4

4. Now you will create a divisibility test for 11.
   a. Show the number 143 using only longs and smalls—no flats. Use as many longs as possible. Show what happens if you join as many smalls as possible to a long. How can you see at a glance that 143 is divisible by 11?
   b. Create a test for divisibility by 11. Explain your thinking.
   c. How and why will your test work with four-digit numbers?

Questions and Conversations for #4

» *How many longs remain without an extra cube?* Because there are 14 longs and 3 smalls, there are 11 longs left without an extra cube.

» *How can you make groups of eleven using these longs?* Reimagine them as 10 groups of eleven instead of 11 groups of ten. (Then you will have a total of 13 groups of eleven.)

» *How can you predict the number of remaining longs by looking at the numeral 143?* Calculate $14-3$, because 3 (the ones digit) is the number of smalls, and 14 (from the first two digits) is the number of longs.

Solution for #4

Solution for a. Show 143 as 14 longs and 3 smalls. When you join the 3 smalls (ones) to 3 of the longs, $14-3=11$ longs are left without an extra cube. This leaves 3 groups of eleven and 11 groups of ten. You can rearrange the 11 groups of ten into 10 groups of eleven, which makes a total of 13 groups of 11. This means that 143 is divisible by 11.

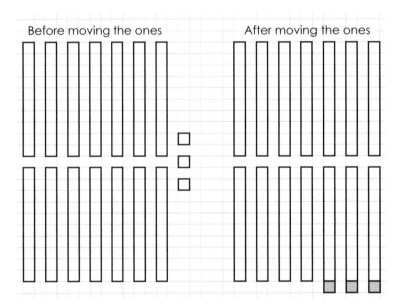

Solution for b. Divisibility test for 11: Subtract the ones digit from the number formed by the remaining digits. This gives you the number of longs left without an extra small. The original number is divisible by 11 if this difference is divisible by 11.

Solution for c. The test still works for 4-digit (and larger) numbers. You will just have more groups of ten to begin with. For example, 5327 has 532 longs and 7 smalls. When you join the 7 smalls to longs, there are $532-7=525$ longs left.

You can repeat the test to see if 525 is divisible by 11: 525 has 52 longs and 5 smalls. $52-5=47$. There are 47 longs left. Because 47 is not divisible by 11, these groups of ten can't be rearranged into a whole number of groups of eleven. 525 is not divisible by 11, so neither is 5327!

STAGE 2

Problem #5

5. Choose one or both of the approaches in parts a and b to create a divisibility test for 7. Use the number 154 to illustrate your thinking process.

   a. Transfer some smalls to or from each long.

   b. Double the number that you're testing by doubling the number of longs and smalls. Then group the longs into pairs and join a small to as many pairs as possible.

   c. These two methods lead to different tests. Tell which test you prefer and why.

> *Teacher's Note.* Students may gradually start drawing simpler diagrams. For example, they might just show longs as line segments and cubes as dots. Some students may even begin to use algebraic notation.
>
> These representations are more abstract than the pictures we've been drawing because they don't show individual cubes. Students should always use representations that are meaningful for them. If they choose these more abstract ones, they should be able to connect them to the more concrete pictures that we've been drawing.

Questions and Conversations for #5

Choice *a*:

» *How many blocks should you move to or from each long?* Think about how to make groups of 7.

Choice *b*:

» *What happens to a number's divisibility by 7 when you double it?* It remains the same. Can you see why? Examples: Because 91 is divisible by 7, so is 182. Because 113 is not divisible by 7, neither is 226.

» *Why do you double the number of longs and smalls before pairing the longs?* This guarantees that you will have an even number of longs to form pairs.

» *Why do you move a small over to each pair that you can?* This forms groups of 21, which contain three groups of 7.

» *How can you determine the number of pairs of longs by looking at the numeral 154?* The first two digits determine the number of pairs—15 in this case. Why does this happen?

» *How can you determine from the numeral 154 how many smalls there will be before you begin joining them to the pairs?* Because you have doubled the number of smalls, there will be 8 of them—twice as many as the ones digit.

» *How can you determine how many smalls or longs will remain after all possible smalls have been joined to the pairs of longs?* Think carefully about what to subtract. The order in which you subtract will be determined by whether there are more smalls or more pairs of longs remaining.

Solution for #5

Solution for a. 154 has 15 longs and 4 smalls. Move 3 smalls from each long and transfer them to the smalls. (Encourage students to imagine or sketch this picture!)

The 15 longs have turned into 15 groups of seven. But now we have 49 smalls: 3 from each of the 15 longs (45) plus the 4 that we started with! Because 49 has a whole number of groups of seven, 154 is divisible by 7.

How do we get a divisibility test from this? First, we don't have to worry about the longs—they've all been turned into groups of seven! We can just focus on the smalls.

There are 3 smalls from every long, plus the smalls that we started with. So if we began with a longs and b smalls, there are now $3 \cdot a + b$ smalls. If $3 \cdot a + b$ is divisible by 7, so is the original number. If not, then it isn't!

Solution for b. 154 has 15 longs and 4 smalls. Double this to get 30 longs and 8 smalls. Then group the 30 longs into 15 pairs.

Move each of the 8 smalls to a pair of longs. This creates groups of twenty-one (two longs and a small):

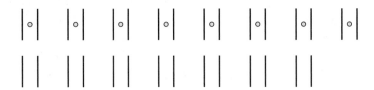

Because the groups of twenty-one have 3 groups of seven, we can ignore them and focus on the remaining 7 pairs. The 7 groups of twenty can be rearranged into 20 groups of seven. Because 154 contains a whole number of groups of seven, it is divisible by 7.

Divisibility test for 7: Let a be the number of longs and b the number of smalls in the original number. If $a - 2 \cdot b$ is divisible by 7, then so is the original number. If not, then it isn't.

Why? a represents both the number of longs in the original number and the number of pairs in the doubled number. $2 \cdot b$ is the number of smalls after you double the number. Therefore, $a - 2 \cdot b$ is the number of pairs of longs left over after you move the cubes to form the groups of twenty-one.

Some students may like the $3 \cdot a + b$ test because it was easier for them to discover. Many may prefer the $a - 2 \cdot b$ test because it is easier to use. $3 \cdot a + b$ often involves messier calculations and more repetitions of the test, especially for large numbers.

STAGE 3

Problem #6

6. Create a divisibility test for 13. Explain your thinking process and justify the procedure.

Questions and Conversations for #6

> » *Why does it help to move only single cubes in or out of the bundles of longs?* This is so that you won't have to multiply the number of bundles by anything. Otherwise, you might be working with some messy calculations. (The number of bundles may already be large.) For example, if you chose option *a* in Problem #5, you may have experienced something like this. Moving three smalls out of each long caused you to multiply the number of longs by 3.

> » *How can you create bundles that allow you to move just one small in or out of them?* Find a multiple of the number for which you are creating the test that has a ones digit of 1 or 9. Can you see why this works?

> » *How many tens should you put in each bundle to create a divisibility test for 13?* You should make bundles of 4 tens. This will create groups of forty. Then you can form a multiple of 13 by removing one small from each bundle.

> » *What can you do to create bundles of four tens?* Quadruple the number of longs and smalls before forming the bundles. (Why doesn't this affect the divisibility by 13?)

> **Teacher's Note.** Students can benefit from exploring more examples of the $a - 2 \cdot b$ test. They will discover that sometimes you subtract in reverse: $2 \cdot b - a$ (if there are extra smalls remaining instead of longs). They may also want to investigate what happens if you don't double the number of longs and smalls at the beginning. Try it in cases where you begin with an even or an odd number of longs.

Solution for #6

Divisibility test for 13: If $a + 4 \cdot b$ is divisible by 13, so is the original number. If not, then it isn't. Students' explanations should show that they formed bundles of 4 longs and removed a small from each one to create groups of 39 (3 groups of thirteen).

Problem #7

7. Describe a general procedure for creating divisibility tests. Explain how to use it to find a test for 17. For what types of numbers can you create a test like this?

Questions and Conversations for #7

» *The type of process you developed in Problem #6 will not work to create tests for numbers with a ones digit of 5. Why not? What other "last digits" won't work?* If a number has a final digit of 5, it won't be possible to find a multiple that has a final digit of 1 or 9. You will have a similar problem with even numbers.

Solution for #7

Divisibility test for n: Find a multiple of n that is one more or one less than a multiple of 10. This makes it possible to shift just one small in or out of each bundle to create a whole number of groups of n.

For example, to create a test for 17, notice that $17 \cdot 3 = 51$, which is one more than 50. Form bundles of 5 and move a small into each. This results in an $a - 5 \cdot b$ test.

This general type of process will work to test numbers whose ones digits are 1, 3, 7, or 9. These are the only numbers that can have a multiple that is one greater or one less than a multiple of 10.

Problem #8

8. There is a test for divisibility by 11 that is especially helpful for large numbers. Use these tables to help you develop this test. Explain your thinking and justify your procedure based on patterns in these tables.

	Divided by 11
9	$0.\overline{81}$
99	9
999	$90.\overline{81}$
9999	909
99,999	$9090.\overline{81}$
999,999	90,909
9,999,999	$909,090.\overline{81}$

	Divided by 11
11	1
101	$9.\overline{18}$
1001	91
10,001	$909.\overline{18}$
100,001	9091
1,000,001	$90,909.\overline{18}$
10,000,001	909,091

Note. There are many fascinating patterns to explore here. For now, focus on the parts that can help you create the divisibility test.

Questions and Conversations for #8

» *What patterns do you see in the numbers that are divisible by 11?* Every alternate number within each table is divisible by 11. When a number in one table is divisible by 11, the corresponding number in the other table is not.

» *How do the numbers in the left columns relate to place values?* They are all 1 greater or 1 less than a power of 10.

» *How can you move smalls in and out of each place value group in order to create groups that are always multiples of 11?* You will have to move a small into the groups of 10, 1000, 100,000, and out of the groups of 100, 10,000, and 1,000,000.

Solution for #8

This divisibility test for 11 is based on alternately adding and subtracting the digits of the original number. (Example: $a - b + c - d + e$ for a five-digit numeral.) This works because you must alternately move smalls in or out of powers of 10 ($10+1$, $100-1$, $1000+1$, $10,000-1$, etc.) to create groups that are divisible by 11.

WRAP UP

Share Strategies

Let students share their reasoning about why the divisibility tests work and how they developed strategies for finding new ones. This is a great opportunity for them to practice expressing complex ideas clearly using correct vocabulary.

Summarize

Answer any remaining questions that students have. Summarize key points:

» We can use place value to analyze and create divisibility tests. Most of these tests involve moving cubes in and out of place value groups to form multiples of the numbers we are creating the test for. By moving single cubes, we usually get tests that are more practical because they involve working with smaller numbers that can be calculated mentally.

» A single number can have many divisibility tests.

» We can use pictures, diagrams, and algebraic symbols to represent our thinking about place value and divisibility tests.

Further Exploration

Ask students to think of ways to continue or extend this exploration. Here are some possibilities:

» Create divisibility tests for larger numbers. Do you think these tests are useful?

» When and how can you create tests for composite numbers using tests for their factors? For example, can you create a divisibility test for 33 using the tests for 3 and 11? (Hint: It helps to choose factors that have a greatest common factor of 1. Why?)

» If you have completed the "Torran Math" exploration, try developing Torran divisibility tests! Remember that their place value blocks look different than ours. How does this affect their tests?

» Continue exploring patterns in the table from Problem #8. What causes the patterns? Do you see similar patterns when you divide by numbers other than 11? What about when you divide other collections of numbers by 11?

» Develop your computational fluency with these divisibility tests. Choose large numbers to test, using mental math as much as possible. Work for speed and accuracy. Check your predictions by dividing the numbers on a calculator.

» Explore patterns that arise when you use divisibility tests. For example, apply the divisibility test for 13 to the numbers 13, 26, 39, 52, 65, 78, etc. Are there patterns in the values of $a + 4 \cdot b$?

Exploration 6

Visualizing Decimal Multiplication

INTRODUCTION

Materials

» Graph paper (to draw diagrams of Base Ten blocks)

Prior Knowledge

» Use Base Ten blocks to represent whole numbers and decimals.
» Use decimal place value to name numbers in multiple ways.
» Know a procedure for multiplying whole numbers.
» Know what it means to square a number (Stage 3).

Learning Goals

» Understand why decimal multiplication procedures work.
» Analyze connections between different decimal multiplication procedures.
» Create real-world stories to match decimal multiplication situations.
» Visualize the commutative ("turn around") property for decimal multiplication.
» Analyze algebraic representations of multiplication patterns (Stage 3).
» Connect grouping models to area models of decimal multiplication (Stage 3).
» Communicate complex mathematical ideas clearly.
» Persist in solving challenging problems.

Launching the Exploration

Purpose and motivation. To students: Procedures for multiplying whole numbers and decimals are very similar. In this exploration, whether or not you know rules for "where to put the decimal," you will start fresh, pretending that you've never heard them. You may even discover some rules of your own! The main goals are not speed and accuracy, but depth of understanding and flexible thinking.

Understanding the problem. Look through the exploration to help students see the big picture. In Stage 1, they use Base Ten blocks to explore the meaning of decimal multiplication. In Stage 2, students analyze various multiplication procedures—why they work and how they are connected. Finally, in Stage 3, they express some of their new knowledge in algebraic language and use this to explore a surprising pattern.

If students already know procedures for multiplying decimals, challenge them to pretend that they had never been taught them. Invite them instead to imagine that they are the first people ever to study these ideas. Their job is to use their knowledge of place value to explore and maybe even invent new processes!

As students begin to work, if they have trouble understanding what "1.4 groups" means, ask them to think of what 1 group, 2 groups, and $1\frac{1}{2}$ groups of 3 would look like.

Teacher's Note. In our work, we will agree that $a \cdot b$ represents b groups of a, while $b \cdot a$ stands for a groups of b. In other words, the first factor will stand for the size of each group, and the second one for the number of groups.

STUDENT HANDOUT

Stage 1

1. This diagram shows 2 groups of 3 flats. It has a value of 6, and it represents the number sentence $3 \cdot 2 = 6$.

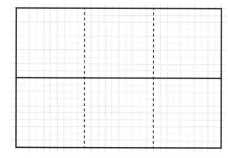

   a. On graph paper, change the diagram to show 1.4 groups of 3 flats. What is the new value and number sentence for your diagram? Use your drawing to explain.

   b. Write a story problem to match this situation.

   c. How can your diagram represent 3 groups of 1.4 flats instead? Explain, and then create a story to fit this situation.

2. Make a diagram showing 1.7 groups of 2.3 flats. Find the value, write a number sentence, and create a story. Explain how to connect all of your answers to your drawing.

3. Adsila, Spencer, and Miriam each have a different strategy to find the value of $2.3 \cdot 1.7$. Use your drawing in Problem #2 to show or explain why each person's strategy makes sense.

   Adsila: $2.3 + 1.61$ Spencer: $3.4 + 0.51$ Miriam: $2 + 1.4 + 0.3 + 0.21$

4. How can you change the way you interpret your diagram so that it represents $23 \cdot 17$ instead? Explain.

5. This is a "cross-hatch" diagram. How does it show the expression $2.3 \cdot 1.7$? How can you use it to find the answer? Explain.

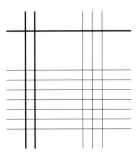

6. Make two diagrams, one cross-hatch and one with Base Ten blocks, for $4.6 \cdot 5.2$. Explain how to use your diagrams to calculate $4.6 \cdot 5.2$. Describe the connections between your two diagrams.

7. Here are two more diagrams that can be used to show $4.6 \cdot 5.2$. (The second diagram is an example of "lattice multiplication.") Study them and explain: How you can use them to find the answer? Why do they work? Connect your explanations to the Base Ten blocks and the crosshatch diagrams.

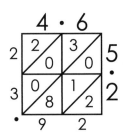

Show one or two other pairs of numbers that you could multiply using the first diagram. How would this work? Explain.

Stage 3

8. Choose a pair of positive numbers a and b (in decimal form) that has a sum of 1. Then evaluate the algebraic expressions $a^2 + b$ and $b^2 + a$. Choose a second pair of numbers satisfying the same condition and repeat. Choose more pairs to test if you like. What do you observe?

9. Select one of your pairs. On graph paper, use these numbers to draw one diagram (with Base Ten blocks) for $a^2 + b$ and one for $b^2 + a$. The picture below is a guide for making one of your drawings. Don't assume that a must be greater than b. (The bottom side of the diagram below should be 10 squares long on your graph paper.) Explain how your diagrams show the expressions and the answer.

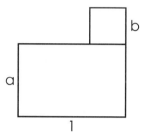

10. Use your diagrams (or make new ones) to explain why your observation in Problem #8 is true whenever a and b have a sum of 1.

11. Use the same kinds of diagrams to create two more algebraic expressions that are equivalent to $a^2 + b$ and $b^2 + a$ whenever $a + b = 1$. Substitute some numbers to test your expressions.

TEACHER'S GUIDE

STAGE 1

Problem #1

1. This diagram shows 2 groups of 3 flats. It has a value of 6, and it represents the number sentence $3 \cdot 2 = 6$.

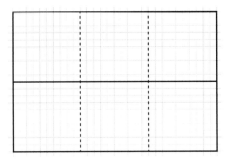

a. On graph paper, change the diagram to show 1.4 groups of 3 flats. What is the new value and number sentence for your diagram? Use your drawing to explain.

b. Write a story problem to match this situation.

c. How can your diagram represent 3 groups of 1.4 flats instead? Explain, and then create a story to fit this situation.

Questions and Conversations for #1

This section contains ideas for conversations, mainly in the form of questions that students may ask or that you may pose to them. Be sure to allow students to do most of the thinking and talking!

» *The flats represent one unit. What do the longs and smalls stand for?* The longs represent 0.1 units and the smalls stand for 0.01 units.

» *What does 1 group of three look like? 2 groups of three? 1.5 groups of three?* One group of three could be the top row of flats in the original picture, 2 groups of three are the entire picture, and 1.5 groups of three are halfway between these.

» *How can you show 0.4 groups of three? How can you use this to create 1.4 groups?* You can begin by splitting one group of three into 10 equal parts.

» *What real-world quantities make sense to use with the number 1.4 in your story?* Quantities that can be split into equal parts or measured rather than counted (e.g., distances, portions of food servings, times, etc.) often work well.

» *Does one number in each story have units of one quantity per another?* It probably does. For 1.4 groups of 3, the number 3 is likely to have this type of unit. For 3 groups of 1.4, it will be the number 1.4.

Solution for #1

There are three flats with a total value of 3, and twelve longs (shaded) with a total value of 12 tenths, or 1 and 2 tenths. The total value of the diagram is 3 plus four tenths of 3, or $3+1.2=4.2$.

This diagram represents the multiplication sentence $3 \cdot 1.4 = 4.2$.

> **Teacher's Note.** Students' diagrams may look different than the ones shown here. This is fine as long as they have the same value and students can explain their meanings. If students have a variety of drawings, ask them to compare them and discuss advantages and disadvantages of each.

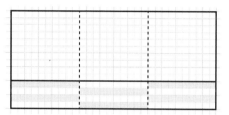

A sample story for 1.4 groups of 3: A sample of dog shampoo costs $3 per ounce. What is the cost of a 1.4 ounce sample of the shampoo? Answer: $4.20

This second diagram represents 3 groups of 1.4:

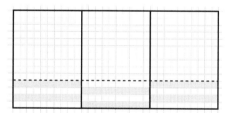

It looks the same as the first one except that it is decomposed differently. Two bold vertical segments separate the diagram into 3 groups of 1.4. These replace the original horizontal segment that separated the flats from the longs. You are likely to find its value by adding $1.4+1.4+1.4=4.2$.

A sample story for 3 groups of 1.4: Chantal rides her bike 1.4 miles to school each day. There are only 3 days of school in the week before spring break. How many miles does she ride to school that week? Answer: 4.2 miles

Problem #2

2. Make a diagram showing 1.7 groups of 2.3 flats. Find the value, write a number sentence, and create a story. Explain how to connect all of your answers to your drawing.

Questions and Conversations for #2

» *What makes this diagram more challenging to draw?* Because both numbers are decimals, you begin with a fractional number of flats.

» *What kinds of visual strategies can you use to see the value of your diagram?* The least efficient strategy is probably to count every small to determine the number of hundredths! If your diagram is rectangular, you can speed this up by counting the number of smalls in its length and width and then multiplying. A more common approach is to split the diagram into parts, find the value of each part, and add them together.

Solution for #2

This diagram shows 1.7 groups of 2.3. It has a value of 3.91 units. The diagram represents the multiplication sentence $2.3 \cdot 1.7 = 3.91$.

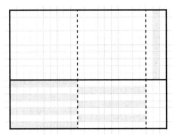

We can decompose the diagram into flats, longs, and smalls to see the value:

2 flats (ones)	2 ones	0 tenths	0 hundredths
17 longs (tenths)	1 one	7 tenths	0 hundredths
21 smalls (hundredths)	0 ones	2 tenths	1 hundredth
TOTAL	3 ones	9 tenths	1 hundredth

A sample story for 1.7 groups of 2.3: A square yard of fabric weighs 2.3 ounces. How much will 1.7 square yards of the fabric weigh? Answer: 3.91 ounces

Teacher's Note. Students' stories may give them new ideas for diagrams and calculation strategies. If so, be sure to allow them to share and discuss these!

Problem #3

3. Adsila, Spencer, and Miriam each have a different strategy to find the value of $2.3 \cdot 1.7$. Use your drawing in Problem #2 to show or explain why each person's strategy makes sense.

Adsila: $2.3 + 1.61$ Spencer: $3.4 + 0.51$ Miriam: $2 + 1.4 + 0.3 + 0.21$

Questions and Conversations for #3

» *How can strategies for finding the values in Problem #2 help you?* The three students are using strategies that involve finding the values of different parts of the diagram and adding them together.

Solution for #3

Adsila decomposed 1.7 as $1 + 0.7$, creating two groups with values of 2.3 and 1.61. Spencer decomposed 2.3 as $2 + 0.3$, creating two groups with values of 3.4 and 0.51. Miriam decomposed both numbers, creating four groups with values of $2, 1.4, 0.3$ and 0.21.

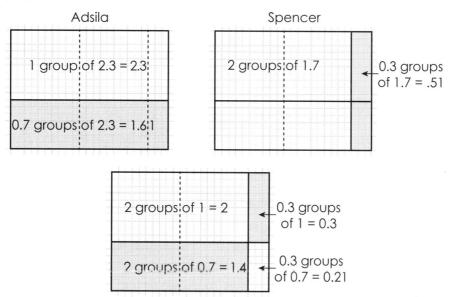

Problem #4

4. How can you change the way you interpret your diagram so that it represents $23 \cdot 17$ instead? Explain.

Questions and Conversations for #4

» *What values do the flats, longs, and smalls represent now?* They will all represent whole number amounts.

Teacher's Note. If students know the traditional algorithm for multiplying two-digit numbers, ask them to try it twice, once with each number on top. Adsila's and Spencer's strategies will appear in their work! Some students may know the *partial products* algorithm. Miriam's strategy will show up in their work.

Solution for #4

To make the diagram represent $23 \cdot 17$, you just have to let flats stand for 100 units instead of 1. Then longs will stand for 10 units and smalls will represent 1 unit. The value becomes 391 instead of 3.91.

STAGE 2

Problem #5

5. This is a "cross-hatch" diagram. How does it show the expression $2.3 \cdot 1.7$? How can you use it to find the answer? Explain.

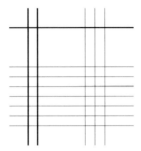

Questions and Conversations for #5

» *What do the dark and the light segments stand for?* The dark segments represent ones and the light segments stand for tenths.

» *What does it represent when the various combinations of segments intersect?*

Dark with dark:	ones · ones	ones
Dark with light:	ones · tenths	tenths
Light with light:	tenths · tenths	hundredths

» *What does it tell you when you count the intersections of segments?* It tells you how many of each place value you have.

Solution for #5

There are 2 dark-dark intersections that represent 2 ones (ones · ones), 3 dark-light intersections for 3 tenths (ones · tenths), 14 light-dark intersections for 14 tenths (tenths · ones), and 21 light-light intersections that stand for 21 hundredths (tenths · tenths). (Notice how the dark-light and light-dark intersections both represent tenths and line up along a diagonal of the crosshatch diagram.)

You can rename these to get

2 ones		
	3 tenths	
1 one	4 tenths	
	2 tenths	1 hundredth
3 ones	9 tenths	1 hundredth

The answer is 3.91.

Problem #6

6. Make two diagrams, one cross-hatch and one with Base Ten blocks, for $4.6 \cdot 5.2$. Explain how to use your diagrams to calculate $4.6 \cdot 5.2$. Describe the connections between your two diagrams.

Questions and Conversations for #6

» *How can you fit such a large diagram on graph paper?* Now that you've had some experience, you may not need to create a diagram that shows each individual long and small—and you may not need graph paper. Can you think of a way to show the "big picture" without all of the details?

» *What does it mean to connect the two diagrams?* Look for something in common between the procedures when you use them to find the value. Try applying Miriam's strategy (see Problem #3) to your Base Ten diagram. Compare the results to the intersections in your crosshatch diagram.

Solution for #6

It's not very practical to show all the longs and smalls for the base-ten diagram. You'll have to use your experience to imagine them!

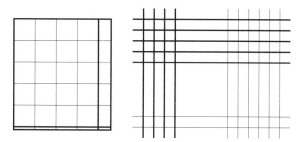

20 flats (ones)	2 tens	0 ones	0 tenths	0 hundredths
8 longs (tenths)	0 tens	0 ones	8 tenths	0 hundredth
30 longs (tenths)	0 tens	3 ones	0 tenths	0 hundredths
12 smalls (hundredths)	0 tens	0 ones	1 tenth	2 hundredths
TOTAL	2 tens	3 ones	9 tenths	2 hundredths

The answer is 23.92.

The 20 flats match the 20 dark-dark intersections, the 30 longs match 30 dark-light intersections, the 8 longs match 8 light-dark intersections, and the 12 smalls match the 12 light-light intersections. Again, the dark-light and light-dark intersections represent the same place value (tenths) and line up diagonally from the lower left to the upper right of the crosshatch diagram!

Problem #7

7. Here are two more diagrams that can be used to show $4.6 \cdot 5.2$. (The second diagram is an example of "lattice multiplication.") Study them and explain: How you can use them to find the answer? Why do they work? Connect your explanations to the Base Ten blocks and the crosshatch diagrams.

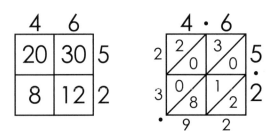

Show one or two other pairs of numbers that you could multiply using the first diagram. How would this work? Explain.

Questions and Conversations for #7

» *In the first diagram, what place values are associated with the numbers in each box?* The 30 and the 8 represent tenths. Can you see why? What place values are associated with the 20 and the 12?

» *How can you combine all of these values to produce an answer?* You can add the four values together, but it may help to rename some of them first. For example, you can rename 30 tenths as 3 ones.

» *How do the contents of the boxes in the two diagrams compare?* The numerals look the same, but diagonal segments separate the digits in the second (lattice multiplication) diagram.

» *How do you obtain the numbers below and to the left of the box in the lattice multiplication diagram?* Try adding the numbers along the diagonals.

» *How can you attach a place value to each digit inside the lattice multiplication box?* You can do this by renaming the numbers in the boxes in the first diagram. For example, you can name 30 tenths as 3 ones and 0 tenths.

» *How are the place values of the digits arranged in the lattice multiplication diagram?* They line up along the diagonals.

Solution for #7

The numbers on the outside of the rectangle are just the digits of the numbers you are multiplying. Each box inside the rectangle is the product of the digits in its row and column. These products match the number of flats, longs, or smalls in the Base Ten diagram, and the number of intersections in each region of the crosshatch diagram.

In order to use this diagram to find the value of $4.6 \cdot 5.2$, you just need to take account of the place values. For example, the top left box shows 4 ones $\cdot$ 5 ones = 20 ones.

The lattice multiplication diagram takes this one step further. The diagonal lines separate the numerals into their component digits. This organizes things so that each diagonal represents a certain place value! You can just add down the diagonals (regrouping when needed) to get the answer.

You can also multiply something like $46 \cdot 52$ with this diagram. Each row, column, and diagonal just stands for a different place value.

STAGE 3

Problem #8

8. Choose a pair of positive numbers a and b (in decimal form) that has a sum of 1. Then evaluate the algebraic expressions $a^2 + b$ and $b^2 + a$. Choose a second pair of numbers satisfying the same condition and repeat. Choose more pairs to test if you like. What do you observe?

Questions and Conversations for #8

» *What does it mean to evaluate an algebraic expression?* The root word is *value*. Substitute your numbers into the expressions and then calculate their values.

Solution for #8

Sample responses, using $a = 0.3$, $b = 0.7$ and $a = 0.42$, $b = 0.58$:
First pair:
$$a^2 + b = 0.3^2 + 0.7 = 0.09 + 0.7 = 0.79$$
$$b^2 + a = 0.7^2 + 0.3 = 0.49 + 0.3 = 0.79$$

Second pair:
$$a^2 + b = 0.42^2 + 0.58 = 0.1764 + 0.58 = 0.7564$$
$$b^2 + a = 0.58^2 + 0.42 = 0.3364 + 0.42 = 0.7564$$

The answer within each pair is the same!

Problem #9

Select one of your pairs. On graph paper, use these numbers to draw one diagram (with Base Ten blocks) for $a^2 + b$ and one for $b^2 + a$. The picture below is a guide for making one of your drawings. Don't assume that a must be greater than b. (The bottom side of the diagram below should be

10 squares long on your graph paper.) Explain how your diagrams show the expressions and the answer.

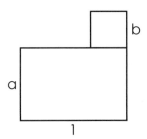

Questions and Conversations for #9

» *What will a^2 look like in your diagram?* It will look like a square with sides of length *a* (whatever value you chose for *a*).

» *The length of the bottom side of the sample diagram is 1. What is the length of the right side? Why?* See the diagram. It is also 1 because it is made from two segments with lengths *a* and *b*, and you were asked to choose your values of *a* and *b* so that $a + b = 1$.

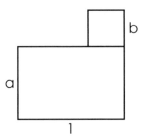

» *Can you use a concept from geometry to represent the value of your diagram?* Yes, the values of all of our Base Ten diagrams are equal to their areas.

» *What happens if you choose a pair of values that does not have a sum of 1?* Try it! Are the values of the two expressions still equal? What happens to the side lengths in your drawing?

Solution for #9

Because both diagrams have the same shape and size, they have the same value (0.79). $a + b$ must equal 1 so that the nonsquare rectangle in each diagram has a side length of 1. This makes it possible to create the regions with the values of 0.7 and 0.3. (Change 0.3 to 0.4 and watch what goes wrong!)

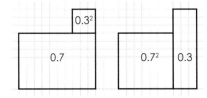

Problem #10

9. Use your diagrams (or make new ones) to explain why your observation in Problem #8 is true whenever a and b have a sum of 1.

> **Teacher's Note.** Help students connect the idea of "groups" to the concept of area. For example, 0.3^2 can represent the area of a square having side lengths of 0.3. It can also stand for 3 tenths of a group of 0.3.

Questions and Conversations for #10

» *How can you show that your observation is true in general without testing all pairs of numbers that have a sum of 1?* Use variables in your diagram.

» *Can you decompose your diagrams so that they show the expressions $a^2 + b$ and $b^2 + a$?* Yes, there are ways to do this. Experiment. Look at how you drew the diagrams for the numbers you chose earlier.

Solution for #10

The diagrams show that you can put the squares and rectangles together in two different ways to create the same shape. The left figure has an area of $b^2 + a$ while the right one has an area of $a^2 + b$. We use variables to show that the specific values of a and b don't matter as long as their sum is 1. This last condition is necessary so that the areas of the nonsquare rectangles are a and b respectively.

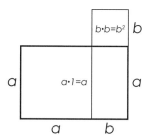 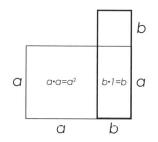

Problem #11

10. Use the same kinds of diagrams to create two more algebraic expressions that are equivalent to $a^2 + b$ and $b^2 + a$ whenever $a + b = 1$. Substitute some numbers to test your expressions.

Questions and Conversations for #11

» *Can you decompose your diagram into more than two parts?* Yes, you may be able obtain a new algebraic expression by splitting it into three parts.

» *What happens if your diagram sits inside a square with side lengths of 1 unit?* You may be able to develop new algebraic expressions by removing a portion of the square to obtain the original diagram.

Solution for #11

If you consider all three parts of the diagram separately, you obtain the expression $a^2 + a \cdot b + b^2$:

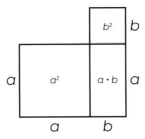

Testing this expression with the same pairs gives

$$0.3^2 + (0.3)(0.7) + 0.7^2 = 0.09 + 0.21 + 0.49 = 0.79$$

$$0.42^2 + (0.42)(0.58) + 0.58^2 = 0.1764 + 0.2436 + 0.3364 = 0.7564$$

You can also think of the diagram as a square (side lengths of $a + b$) with a rectangle removed. The large square has a value of $(a + b)^2$, but this is just equal to 1 (because $a + b = 1$)! You obtain the value of the original shape by removing the upper left rectangle with the value of $a \cdot b$. This results in the expression $1 - a \cdot b$.

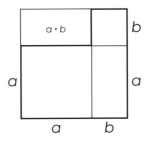

If you test this, you get the same results as before!

$$1 - (0.3)(0.7) = 1 - 0.21 = 0.79$$

$$1 - (0.42)(0.58) = 1 - 0.2436 = 0.7564$$

WRAP UP

Share Strategies

As students share their thinking from Stage 1, check that they are really focusing on forming groups. Picturing 1.4 groups of 3 is different than thinking "length = 3 and width = 1.4". To understand the meaning of decimal (or fraction) multiplication thoroughly, students should see how the idea of area connects to and emerges naturally from forming groups.

Have students share and critique each other's stories. Do they reflect a real understanding of fractional groups and multiplication? Are the quantities realistic in size and precision? Are the stories worded correctly?

Summarize

Answer any remaining questions that students have. Review and compare all of the multiplication processes that students have learned. They are all based on the *distributive property*, which involves decomposing one or both factors, and finding the values of the different parts. *Discuss* how the new processes connect to any procedures they may already know.

Further Exploration

Ask students to think of ways to continue or extend this exploration. Here are some possibilities:

» Create your own decimal multiplication expressions with more digits. Apply each of the strategies you learned in this activity. Pay attention to how the strategies connect. Create stories for your expressions.

» Continue exploring the procedures and strategies from this activity. Look for new ways to organize the place value information. Can you find "shortcuts" to make the methods more efficient? (If so, be sure you understand why they work!)

» Can you find a quick procedure to place the decimal point correctly in the lattice multiplication method? (Hint: How can you find where the "ones" diagonal is?)

» Show how you could use the first diagram in Problem #7 to find the value of an expression like $4.06 \cdot 520$. (Do this without inserting zeros or changing the diagram in any way.)

» Extend the ideas in this activity to explore ways to rewrite algebraic expressions. Each time you rewrite an expression, test it by substituting a variety of numbers. Here are some expressions you could explore:

$$a \cdot (x + y) \qquad (m + n) \cdot m \qquad (x + 1) \cdot (y + 1)$$

$$(a + x) \cdot (b + y) \qquad (a + b + c) \cdot (x + y + z)$$

Exploration 7
Think Like a Torran!

INTRODUCTION

Materials
- » Graph paper

Prior Knowledge
- » Complete Exploration 2: Torran Math.
- » Complete Stage 1 of Exploration 6: Visualizing Decimal Multiplication (recommended).
- » Complete Stage 1 or more of Exploration 5: Creating Divisibility Tests (for Stage 3 only).

Learning Goals
- » Create and justify algorithms in a different numeration system.
- » Represent and perform operations on numbers less than 1 in a different numeration system.
- » Explore, extend, and analyze patterns in numerals and procedures in a different numeration system.
- » Communicate complex mathematical ideas clearly.
- » Persist in solving challenging problems.

Launching the Exploration

Motivation and purpose. To students: In this exploration, you will pretend to be a Torran mathematician. All numerals will be written in the Torran system. Numbers will usually be written in word form. Your challenge is to do as the title suggests—really think like a Torran! Try not to use Earth numerals in your thinking except to check your work.

Understanding the problem. Remind students that the Torran place value system is based on groups of four. The value of each place is four times as large as the previous one: four, sixteen, sixty-four, etc. Use an example or two to review how this causes Torran numerals to look different than ours. For example, the Torran numeral 213 represents the number *thirty-nine* because it means 2 groups of sixteen, 1 group of four, and 3 groups of one. In Earth symbols, this looks like $2 \cdot 16 + 1 \cdot 4 + 3 \cdot 1 = 32 + 4 + 3 = 39$.

Look through the entire activity with students to help them see the big picture. In Stage 1, they use place value blocks to help them create Torran procedures for adding, subtracting, and multiplying numbers. In Stage 2, they work with a Torran version of decimals. In Stage 3, students who completed Exploration 5: Discovering Divisibility Tests will have a chance to create Torran divisibility tests!

As students begin work, check that they complete the tables in Problem #1 correctly. Help them get started using Torran place value blocks if necessary.

Teacher's Note. To make the activity more "authentically Torran," you could suggest that students rewrite the numerals in the problem numbers! For example, in Stage 1, the problems would be numbered 1, 2, 3, 4, 10, 11, and 12 instead of 1, 2, 3, 4, 5, and 6. If they do this, you will probably want to renumber them for yourself as well in the "Questions and Conversations" and "Solutions" sections.

STUDENT HANDOUT

Stage 1

1. Copy and complete the Torran addition and multiplication tables.

+	0	1	2	3
0				
1		2		
2			10	
3				

•	0	1	2	3
0				
1		1		
2			10	
3				

2. Show how to use Torran place value blocks to find $203 + 13$. Then create and describe a procedure for doing the calculation without the blocks. Use place value concepts to explain why your procedure works.

3. Repeat Problem #2 for $203 - 13$.

4. Describe a Torran procedure for making a number four times as large. Extend this idea to other powers of 4. Explain why your procedures work.

5. Create a procedure to calculate $23 \cdot 3$. Show each step of your method and explain why it works. Your explanation should use Torran place value.

6. Repeat Problem #5 for the calculation $32 \cdot 13$.

Stage 2

The Torrans place a dot (a "tetrimal" point) directly below the ones digit to help them show numbers less than one. (If there is no tetrimal point, the rightmost digit is in the ones place.) For example, instead of writing "0.3," the Torrans would write "0 3." This shows that the 0 is in the ones place.

7. How do you think the Torrans would write numerals for four, one fourth, sixteen, one sixteenth, sixty-four, and one sixty-fourth? Show the tetrimal point in all six numerals. What patterns do you observe? What causes them?

8. Show a procedure the Torrans could use to calculate $32 \cdot 13$. Use Torran place value to explain why your method works.

9. Find an efficient way for Torrans to divide a number by four. Extend your method to divide by other powers of four. Explain why your procedures work.

10. Find half of 2310. Continue taking half of each answer you get until you get a value less than one. Show your strategies and explain why they work. Describe any patterns you see and explain what causes them.

Stage 3

11. If you have completed Exploration 5: Creating Divisibility Tests, develop Torran divisibility tests for four, two, and three. Use place value blocks to explain your test for three.

TEACHER'S GUIDE

STAGE 1

Problem #1

1. Copy and complete the Torran addition and multiplication tables.

+	0	1	2	3
0				
1		2		
2			10	
3				

•	0	1	2	3
0				
1		1		
2			10	
3				

Questions and Conversations for #1

This section contains ideas for conversations, mainly in the form of questions that students may ask or that you may pose to them. Be sure to allow students to do most of the thinking and talking!

» *What kinds of patterns do you expect to see in the tables?* Answers are symmetrical across a diagonal line from the upper left to the lower right corners of the table. Entries in the rows and columns of the addition table count by ones. Entries in the multiplication table count by the number on the left (for rows) or top (for columns).

Solution for #1

+	0	1	2	3
0	0	1	2	3
1	1	2	3	10
2	2	3	10	11
3	3	10	11	12

•	0	1	2	3
0	0	0	0	0
1	0	1	2	3
2	0	2	10	12
3	0	3	12	21

Problem #2

2. Show how to use Torran place value blocks to find $203 + 13$. Then create and describe a procedure for doing the calculation without the blocks. Use place value concepts to explain why your procedure works.

Questions and Conversations for #2

» *What do the Torran numerals 203 and 13 look like with their place value blocks?* The rightmost digits tell you the number of smalls. The next digits to the left tell you the number of longs, etc. How do Torran longs and smalls differ from ours?

» *What happens to the place value blocks when you add the numbers?* You combine the blocks for the two numbers.

» *What happens if the number of blocks of any type is greater than or equal to four?* You combine blocks to form a group of a higher place value.

» *Are our Base Ten procedures for addition similar to the Torrans' procedures?* Yes! The place value blocks show you that they can also add numbers for each place value and regroup as needed.

Solution for #2

1. Form 203 and 13 with blocks.

2. Join the blocks.

3. Group four smalls into one long. This leaves 2 flats, 2 longs, and 2 smalls (222).

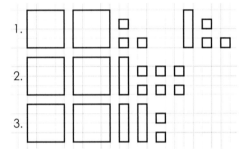

The following method looks like our own traditional algorithm for addition but students may develop many other approaches.

> Add 3 ones + 3 ones to get 12 ones. Rename 12 ones as 1 four and 2 ones. Write a 2 in the ones column and a 1 at the top of the fours column. Add 1 four + 0 fours + 1 four to get 2 fours. Write 2 in the fours column. The sixteens column remains as it is.
>
> $$\begin{array}{r} {}^{1} \\ 203 \\ +13 \\ \hline 222 \end{array}$$

Problem #3

3. Repeat Problem #2 for $203 - 13$.

Questions and Conversations for #3

» *What happens to the blocks when you subtract 13?* You take away 13 blocks (1 long and 3 smalls).

» *What if there aren't enough blocks of the right kind to take away?* Think about what we do on Earth when this happens. (We decompose or break apart blocks of a higher place value to get what we need.)

Solution for #3

1. Show 203 with blocks.

2. Decompose one flat into four longs.

3. Take away 13 (1 long and the 3 smalls).

4. This leaves 1 flat, 3 longs and 0 smalls (130).

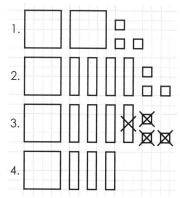

Many students may use the Torran version of our "traditional" subtraction method:

Subtract: 3 ones – 3 ones = 0 ones. Take one group of sixteen and move it to the fours column as 10 (four) groups of four. Subtract: 10 fours – 1 four = 3 fours. Write 1 in the sixteens column.	1 10 2̶03 −13 130

Some students may count backward by 3 ones and then by 1 four (203 → 200 and then 200 → 130).

Problem #4

4. Describe a Torran procedure for making a number four times as large. Extend this idea to other powers of 4. Explain why your procedures work.

Questions and Conversations for #4

» *How can you make 3 smalls four times as large?* One way is to create four groups of 3 smalls. What is another way? (Instead of creating four groups of 3, create 3 groups of four! How does this affect the numeral?)

» *What happens if you start with 20 (2 longs) and make it four times as large?* Instead of having 2 groups of four, you will have 2 groups of sixteen. How does this affect the numeral?

» *Does this remind you of a multiplication process that we use on Earth?* It looks a lot like what happens when we multiply by ten!

Solution for #4

To make the number 3 four times as large, change it from 3 groups of one to 3 groups of four by moving the digit 3 from the ones place to the fours place (30). To make 20 four times as large, move the 2 from the fours to the sixteens place (200).

For any number, move all of its digits one place to the left to make all of their values four times as large.

To make a number sixteen times as large, shift its digits two places to the left (because this multiplies by four twice). To multiply by any power of four, shift its digits a number of places equal to the exponent. For example, to make a number 64 times as large, move its digits three places to the left because $64 = 4^3$. (The Torrans would write this as $1000 = 10^3$!)

Problem #5

5. Create a procedure to calculate $23 \cdot 3$. Show each step of your method and explain why it works. Your explanation should use Torran place value.

Questions and Conversations for #5

» *What does it look like if you show three groups of 23 with Torran place value blocks?* You start with 2 longs and 3 smalls, and then triple each of these. (Try working with the longs and smalls separately. Does this remind you of any strategies we use on Earth?)

Solution for #5

Students might try a method like one they've learned before—perhaps one of these:

Partial Products	Traditional
23	$\overset{2}{2}3$
x3	x3
21	201
120	
201	

Place value blocks can help you understand why these methods work. You can begin by showing 3 groups of 23 (2 longs and 3 smalls).

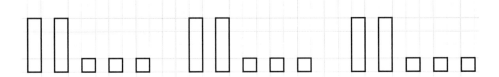

You can combine the three groups of 20 (2 longs) into one flat and 2 longs (120). This represents $20 \cdot 3 = 120$. You can collect the three groups of 3 (3 smalls) to form 2 longs and 1 small (21). This represents $3 \cdot 3 = 21$.

You can combine the remaining four longs to make another flat.

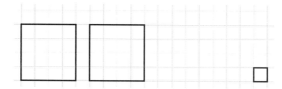

The final result is 2 flats, 0 longs, and 1 small (201).

Both methods involve thinking of $23 \cdot 3$ as $(20 \cdot 3) + (3 \cdot 3)$. Some students might also notice the connection between $20 \cdot 3 = 120$ and $2 \cdot 3 = 12$.

Problem #6

6. Repeat Problem #5 for the calculation $32 \cdot 13$.

Solution for #6

Here are the same two methods for $32 \cdot 13$.

Partial Products	Traditional
32	¹
x13	32
12	x13
210	222
20	320
300	1202
1202	

One way to see why this works this is to arrange the place value blocks in a rectangle. Each row is a group of 32 (3 longs and 2 smalls), and there are 13 rows:

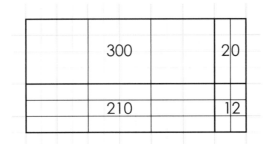

The partial products process shows each piece: $2 \cdot 3$ (12); $30 \cdot 3$ (210); $2 \cdot 10$ (20); and $30 \cdot 10$ (300). In the traditional method, 222 is $210 + 12$ and 320 is $300 + 20$. Add these together at the end to get the total value.

STAGE 2

Problem #7

The Torrans place a dot (a "tetrimal" point) directly below the ones digit to help them show numbers less than one. (If there is no tetrimal point, the rightmost digit is in the ones place.) For example, instead of writing "0.3," the Torrans would write "03." This shows that the 0 is in the ones place.

7. How do you think the Torrans would write numerals for four, one fourth, sixteen, one sixteenth, sixty-four, and one sixty-fourth? Show the tetrimal point in all six numerals. What patterns do you observe? What causes them?

Questions and Conversations for #7

» *Why do you think the Torran word is "tetrimal" instead of "decimal"?* We use "dec-" because it's a prefix for "ten." "Tetr-" is a prefix for "four" and the Torrans group by fours. (Some students may make the connection to the game "Tetris," which uses shapes made of four blocks.)

» *What is the value of the place to the right of the ones digit on Torr?* Suppose that a flat represents 1. What are the values of the longs and smalls?

» *Do you notice any symmetry in the numerals? Why doesn't this happen on Earth?* These Torran numerals show symmetry around the ones place. This isn't as easy to see with Earth numerals because we put the decimal point between places.

Solution for #7

The Torran place values to the right of the ones place are one fourth and one sixteenth. This is because the values of the places keep getting *one fourth* as large as you move to the right.

four: $1\overset{\bullet}{0}$ one fourth: $\overset{\bullet}{0}1$

sixteen: $10\overset{\bullet}{0}$ one sixteenth: $\overset{\bullet}{0}01$

sixty-four: $100\overset{\bullet}{0}$ one sixty-fourth: $\overset{\bullet}{0}001$

Because the 1 is moving one place each time, there is another 0 each time you move to the next row. In each row, the numerals are mirror images. This is because the digit 1 is the same distance from the ones place, but on the opposite side. Our own numerals don't show this perfect symmetry because we put our decimal point between the ones and the tenths places rather than directly at the center of the symmetry—the ones place.

Problem #8

8. Show a procedure the Torrans could use to calculate $3\overset{\bullet}{2}\cdot1\overset{\bullet}{3}$. Use Torran place value to explain why your method works.

Questions and Conversations for #8

» *How does this compare to the calculation in Problem #6?* The digits are the same, but the place values are different.
» *How does this affect how you show the calculation with place value blocks?* You can use the same blocks as before! Just let them represent different values.
» *How could estimation help you?* Think about the nearest whole numbers that each factor is between. For example, on Earth you could estimate that $5.6\cdot9.2$ is between $5\cdot9$ and $6\cdot10$. Why?

Solution for #8

The digits will be 1202, the same as for $3\overset{\bullet}{2}\cdot1\overset{\bullet}{3}$ (see Problem #6) because only the place values have changed. The question is where to put the tetrimal point.

Sample strategy 1: Use estimation to place the tetrimal point. Because $3\overset{\bullet}{2}$ is between 3 and 10, and $1\overset{\bullet}{3}$ is between 1 and 2, $3\overset{\bullet}{2}\cdot1\overset{\bullet}{3}$ must be between $3\cdot1=3$ and $10\cdot2=20$. Because 12 is between these two numbers, the answer must be $1\overset{\bullet}{2}02$.

Sample strategy 2: Count the tetrimal places (just as we can do with decimals). Because there is a total of two places to the right of the tetrimal points in the numbers you are multiplying, there will also be two of them in the answer.

This works because the smallest place value in the answer comes from the smallest place values in the numbers you multiply. These are both fourths. One fourth of one fourth is one sixteenth, so the smallest place value in the answer must be one sixteenth. This means the final digit must be two places to the right of the tetrimal point: $120\overset{\bullet}{2}$.

Problem #9

9. Find an efficient way for Torrans to divide a number by four. Extend your method to divide by other powers of four. Explain why your procedures work.

Questions and Conversations for #9

» *How does this compare to Problem #4?* It still involves the number four, but now you're dividing instead of multiplying. How does this affect what happens to the place values?

Solution for #9

To divide by four, move each digit in the numeral one place to the right. For example, $310 \div 10 = 31$ and $12 \div 10 = 1\overset{\bullet}{2}$. (Remember that 10 is four on Torr!)

This makes sense because moving digits one place to the right makes their values one fourth as large. To divide by other powers of four, move the digits 2 places for sixteen, 3 places for sixty-four, etc., but now you shift them to the right to make the values smaller.

> **Teacher's Note.** We talk about "moving digits" instead of "taking away zeros" or "moving the tetrimal point" in order to focus students' attention on the place value.

> **Teacher's Note for #10.** Students might try to create a long division procedure. This is fine, but they could also draw 2310 with place value blocks and take half of those. As they continue, they should watch for patterns.

Problem #10

10. Find half of 2310. Continue taking half of each answer you get until you get a value less than one. Show your strategies and explain why they work. Describe any patterns you see and explain what causes them.

Solution for #10

Half of 2310 is 1122.

Sample strategy 1: Decompose 2310 into its place value parts: $2310 = 2000 + 300 + 10$. Take half of each part and add them back together: $1000 + 120 + 2 = 1122$. (Why is half of 300 equal to 120? Look at place value blocks to see.)

Sample strategy 2: Double the number and shift the digits one place to the right, $2310 + 2310 = 11220$. When you move the digits, you get 1122.

This works because when you move the digits one place to the right, it makes the number one fourth as large. Doubling it and then taking one fourth of it makes it one half as large. (You could also reverse the order: shift the digits right first, and then double the result.)

If you keep taking half of each number, the list will look like this:

$$2310, 1122, 231, 11\overset{\cdot}{2}2, 2\overset{\cdot}{3}1, 11\overset{\cdot}{2}2, 2\overset{\cdot}{3}1, 1122, 0\overset{\cdot}{2}31.$$

Once you know the first two numbers in the list, there is a faster way! Look to the numeral two steps behind in the list and shift its digits one place to the right. This works because when you take half of a number twice in a row, it becomes one fourth as large.

Problem #11

11. If you have completed Exploration 5: Creating Divisibility Tests, develop Torran divisibility tests for four, two, and three. Use place value blocks to explain your test for three.

Questions and Conversations for #11

» *How do you count by fours in Torran? What kind of skip counting does this remind you of on Earth?* 10, 20, 30, 100, 110, etc. It looks almost like counting by tens on Earth.

» *How do you count by twos in Torran? What kind of skip counting does this remind you of on Earth?* 2, 10, 12, 20, 22, 30, 32, 100, 102, etc. It looks a little like counting by fives on Earth.

» *What happens when you remove 1 small cube from each type of Torran value block?* If you remove 1 cube from a Torran long, there will be 3 smalls left. If you do this with a flat, there will be 33 cubes remaining. Can you explain why this happens and why it is important?

Solution for #11

A number is divisible by four if its Torran numeral ends in 0. It is easy to see this by counting by fours: 10, 20, 30, 100, 110, 120, 130, 200, 210, etc. (When the numeral ends in 0, there are no small place value blocks. You can always decompose what remains into a whole number of groups of four.)

A number is divisible by 2 if its Torran numeral ends in 0 or 2. You see this if you count by twos: 2, 10, 12, 20, 22, 30, 32, 100, 102, 110, 112, 120, 122, etc.

A number is divisible by 3 if the sum of its digits is divisible by 3. To see why, notice that if you take 1 away from a power of four, you always get a number that is divisible by 3. For example, look at the place value blocks to see why $10 - 1 = 3$, $100 - 1 = 33$, and $1000 - 1 = 333$. The numbers, 3, 33, and 333 are all divisible by 3.

If these single blocks are removed from the longs, flats, large cubes, etc., and combined with the smalls (ones) blocks, the number of smalls will be the same as the sum of the digits. If these can be put into a whole number of groups of 3, then so can the original number! If not, then it can't. (Note: You can't "add the digits" to test for divisibility by 3 in every base. Why not? Why does it work for Bases Ten and Four?)

WRAP UP

Share Strategies

Have students share and compare the computational procedures that they developed. Do they all work? Which ones are the easiest to understand? Which ones are the most efficient? Why do they make sense (or not)?

Encourage students to check some of their calculations by seeing if they hold true when you translate the numerals into Base Ten.

Summarize

Answer any remaining questions that students have.

To promote a deeper understanding of place value, draw students' attention to the features of their work that relate to the numbers themselves, and those that are artifacts of the numeration system. For example, lengths of numerals, details of counting patterns, and the numbers of addition and multiplication facts you might be asked to memorize all depend on the numeration system. On the other hand, general procedures such as regrouping, trading, counting place values, and shifting digits might work across place value systems (because they are based on the deeper properties of numbers themselves—commutative, associative, and distributive).

Further Exploration

Ask students to think of ways to continue or extend this exploration. Here are some possibilities:

» Practice doing more Torran calculations to increase your fluency. Use a variety of methods, including those developed by other students.

» Skip count in Torran (by twos, threes, fours, sixteens, halves, fourths, etc.) Look for patterns.

» Perform calculations in other base systems, including some such as Base Twelve or Sixteen.

» Develop a Torran algorithm for division. Explain why it works.

» What would a Torran version of our metric measurement system look like? Invent units for length, mass, and time. Subdivide them in ways that would make it easy to calculate conversions between them.

» How would the Torrans use their place value system to write numbers such as nine sixteenths, three eighths, or one third? Answers: $0\dot{2}1$, $0\dot{1}\dot{2}$, and $0111111\overline{11}$.

» Explore Torran divisibility tests for numbers other than two, three, and four. Use place value blocks to understand and explain why they work. Try inventing divisibility tests for other base systems!

Exploration 8

Extreme Calculations

INTRODUCTION

Materials

- » Scientific calculator (optional)

Prior Knowledge

- » Know the terms *number-word notation*, *standard notation*, *exponential notation*, *scientific notation*, and *order of magnitude*.
- » Complete Levels 1 and 2 of Exploration 4: "Millions, Billions, Trillions . . ."
- » Know how to add and subtract positive and negative integers (recommended).

Learning Goals

- » Analyze and extend patterns to understand powers of 10 for numbers less than or equal to 1.
- » Develop, justify, and apply strategies to multiply and divide powers of 10.
- » Extend understanding of scientific notation to numbers less than 1.
- » Develop, justify, and apply strategies to multiply and divide large and small numbers.
- » Create and solve real-world problems using very large and very small numbers.
- » Explore some properties of exponents.
- » Communicate complex mathematical ideas clearly.
- » Persist in solving challenging problems.

Launching the Exploration

Motivation and purpose. To students: In "Millions, Billions, Trillions . . .," you learned to use scientific notation to work with very large numbers. In this exploration, you will extend this knowledge to very small numbers. Once you have some good calculation strategies at hand, you will apply them to answer and create some "extreme" questions!

Understanding the problem. Look through the entire exploration (or as much as students will be completing) to help them see the big picture. Stage 1 is mainly about relationships among powers of 10 for numbers less than 1. Stage 2 extends students' understanding of scientific notation to small numbers and asks them to apply what they've learned to create and justify their own calculation procedures and to solve problems. Finally, in Stage 3, they create their own "real-life" questions and answer them.

As students begin work, check that they are able to recognize and extend patterns in the number line in Problem #1 in order to prepare them for success with the remainder of the activity.

STUDENT HANDOUT

Stage 1

1. Copy the number line and finish labeling each dot. Describe any patterns you see. Explain how the patterns can help you finish labeling the number line.

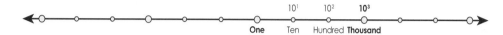

2. Copy and complete the table. Use mental math to find the values in the "Number–Word Notation" column. Use the number line in Problem #1 if it helps.

	Value: Number–Word Notation	Multiplication or Division Sentence: Standard Notation	Multiplication or Division Sentence: Exponential Notation
100 groups of 10,000			
1000 groups of 0.01			
0.01 groups of 100			
0.1 groups of 0.001			
How many groups of 100 are in 10,000?			
Split 100 into 10,000 groups of equal size.			
How many groups of 0.01 are in 1000?			
Split 0.01 into 1,000 groups of equal size.			
How many groups of 0.00001 are in 0.001?			

3. Describe any patterns you see in the number sentences, especially in the final column. Relate the patterns to your mental math strategies.

Exploration 8: Extreme Calculations

Stage 2

Naming a number using its *order of magnitude* (largest place value) has the advantage of giving you a quick idea of its approximate size. (See Exploration 4.) Study these examples carefully to see how you can use order of magnitude to write small numbers in scientific notation.

	Number-Word Notation Using Order of Magnitude	Scientific Notation
0.03	3 hundredths	3×10^{-2}
0.17	1.7 tenths	1.7×10^{-1}
0.000146	1.46 ten-thousandths	1.46×10^{-4}
0.003772	3.772 thousandths	3.772×10^{-3}

4. Complete a table like the one above to write the following numbers in scientific notation. Use the number line from Problem #1 if it helps.

   a. 0.8   b. 0.0013   c. 0.0000972   d. 0.0000056

Find the values in Problems #5–#9 by developing your own strategies based on place value or scientific notation. Avoid using calculators or methods that involve writing out a lot of zeros. Show your work and explain why your strategies make sense.

5. a. 0.03×0.4 b. 0.006×2000 c. $7,000,000 \times 0.12$

6. a. $40 \div 0.02$ b. $0.9 \div 30,000$ c. $0.00012 \div 0.04$

7. If a nation's debt is about 17,000,000,000,000 dollars and the population is about 320,000,000 people, what is each person's approximate share of the debt? (These numbers are close to the figures for the U.S. at the time of this writing.)

8. Dollar bills are about 0.0042 inches thick and Mount Everest is about 348,000 inches tall. Approximately how many dollar bills would you stack to reach the top of Mount Everest?

9. Suppose a hummingbird flaps its wings about once every 0.038 seconds. Given that light travels one mile in about 0.0000054 seconds, about how many miles will light travel in one flap of the hummingbird's wings?

10. Select items from the following data* to create and answer at least three story problems. Show your work or explain your strategies. You may use a calculator, but you should also apply mental math and estimation skills to insure that your results are reasonable.

distance to the nearest star beyond our solar system	4.3 light years**
average distance from the Earth to the Sun	93,000,000 miles
average distance from the Earth to the Moon	240,000 miles
diameter of the Earth	7,900 miles
diameter of a grain of sand (sample)	0.0002 meters
diameter of a red blood cell	0.000007 meters
diameter of a water molecule	0.0000000003 meters
weight of a mosquito (sample)	0.000088 ounces
weight of an African elephant (sample)	7000 pounds
mass of the Empire State Building	300,000,000 kilograms
mass of the Earth	5.97×10^{24} kilograms
one cycle of vibration for the highest note on a piano	0.00024 seconds
time interval for the blink of an eye (sample)	0.3 seconds
total lifetime of the sun	11,000,000,000 years
rate of movement of continental plates (sample)	2 centimeters per year
rate of human hair growth (sample)	0.5 inches per month
current speed of Voyager 1 spacecraft	17.1 kilometers per second
speed of sound	760 miles per hour
speed of light in a vacuum***	299,792,458 meters per second

*Some values are quite variable. These are labeled with the word "sample" and a typical value is shown. Remember that measured values are never exact.

**A light year is the distance that light travels in one year.

***This value is exact because it is a universal constant and the length of a meter is actually defined (in part) by it!

TEACHER'S GUIDE

STAGE 1

Problem #1

1. Copy the number line and finish labeling each dot. Describe any patterns you see. Explain how the patterns can help you finish labeling the number line.

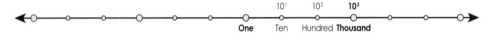

Questions and Conversations for #1

This section contains ideas for conversations, mainly in the form of questions that students may ask or that you may pose to them. Be sure to allow students to do most of the thinking and talking!

» *Why do you think some dots, numerals, and labels are written larger than the others?* It emphasizes the way we group digits by threes. Notice that these exponents are multiples of 3.

» *What does the exponent on the power of 10 tell you about the position of each dot?* It tells you how far you are from the ones place (and in which direction).

» *What happens to the value when you move one dot to the right?* It becomes one tenth as large (divides by 10).

» *Why is 10^{-2} not equal to –100? What is the correct value? Explain.* Decreasing the exponent makes the value smaller but it does not make it negative. The correct value is 0.01. The center of the pattern is at 10^0 (1). If you start there and move two places to the right, you begin at 1 and take one tenth of it twice.

$$1 \div 10 \div 10 = 0.01 \text{ or } 1 \times 0.1 \times 0.1 = 0.01$$

Solution for #1

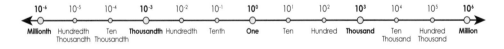

Problem #2

2. Copy and complete the table. Use mental math to find the values in the "Number–Word Notation" column. Use the number line in Problem #1 if it helps.

	Value: Number–Word Notation	Multiplication or Division Sentence: Standard Notation	Multiplication or Division Sentence: Exponential Notation
100 groups of 10,000			
1000 groups of 0.01			
0.01 groups of 100			
0.1 groups of 0.001			
How many groups of 100 are in 10,000?			
Split 100 into 10,000 groups of equal size.			
How many groups of 0.01 are in 1000?			
Split 0.01 into 1,000 groups of equal size.			
How many groups of 0.00001 are in 0.001?			

Questions and Conversations for #2

» *What happens to the size of a number when you multiply it by 10 (100)? What effect does this have on the placement of each digit?* It becomes 10 (100) times as large. Each digit shifts one (two) places to the left.

» *What happens to the size of a number when you divide it by 10 (100)? What effect does this have on the placement of each digit?* It becomes one tenth (one hundredth) as large. Each digit shifts one (two) places to the right.

» *What happens to a number when you divide it by a number between 0 and 1?* It becomes larger.

» *How do the exponents relate to the positions of the digits and how far they move?* The exponent on a power of 10 tells you how far you are from the ones place. If you multiply or divide by a power of 10, it tells you how many places the digits shift. This makes sense because the exponent represents how many times you multiply or divide by 10.

125

Solution for #2

	Value: Number–Word Notation	Multiplication or Division Sentence: Standard Notation	Multiplication or Division Sentence: Exponential Notation
100 groups of 10,000	1 million	$10,000 \times 100 = 1,000,000$	$10^4 \times 10^2 = 10^6$
1000 groups of 0.01	ten	$0.01 \times 1000 = 10$	$10^{-2} \times 10^3 = 10^1$
0.01 groups of 100	one	$100 \times 0.01 = 1$	$10^2 \times 10^{-2} = 10^0$
0.1 groups of 0.001	1 ten-thousandth	$0.001 \times 0.1 = 0.0001$	$10^{-3} \times 10^{-1} = 10^{-4}$
How many groups of 100 are in 10,000?	1 hundred	$10,000 \div 100 = 100$	$10^4 \div 10^2 = 10^2$
Split 100 into 10,000 groups of equal size.	1 hundredth	$100 \div 10,000 = 0.01$	$10^2 \div 10^4 = 10^{-2}$
How many groups of 0.01 are in 1000?	1 hundred-thousand	$1000 \div 0.01 = 100,000$	$10^3 \div 10^{-2} = 10^5$
Split 0.01 into 1000 groups of equal size.	1 hundred thousandth	$0.01 \div 1000 = 0.00001$	$10^{-2} \div 10^3 = 10^{-5}$
How many groups of 0.00001 are in 0.001?	1 hundred	$0.001 \div 0.00001 = 100$	$10^{-3} \div 10^{-5} = 10^2$

Problem #3

3. Describe any patterns you see in the number sentences, especially in the final column. Relate the patterns to your mental math strategies.

Questions and Conversations for #3

» *What happens to the exponents in the final column? What causes this?* The exponents appear to add (for multiplication) or subtract (for division). This just reflects the position and movement of the digit 1.

» *Why are negative exponents associated with rightward position and movement?* This is because our numerals are written so that place values decrease as you move to the right.

Solution for #3

The digit 1 moves in predictable ways. These relate to patterns in the exponents. When you multiply, the exponents add. When you divide, the exponents subtract (in the corresponding order to the division). The reason is that the exponents track the position and movement of the digit 1 relative to the ones place. For example, $10^4 \times 10^2 = 10^6$ shows that the 1 begins four places to the left of the ones, moves two places further to the left, and ends up six places to the left of the ones. Or, $10^2 \times 10^{-3} = 10^{-1}$ shows that the 1 begins two places to the left of the ones, moves three places to the right, and ends up one place to the right of it.

STAGE 2

Problem #4

Naming a number using its *order of magnitude* (largest place value) has the advantage of giving you a quick idea of its approximate size. (See Exploration 4.) Study these examples carefully to see how you can use order of magnitude to write small numbers in scientific notation.

	Number–Word Notation Using Order of Magnitude	Scientific Notation
0.03	3 hundredths	3×10^{-2}
0.17	1.7 tenths	1.7×10^{-1}
0.000146	1.46 ten-thousandths	1.46×10^{-4}
0.003772	3.772 thousandths	3.772×10^{-3}

4. Complete a table like the one above to write the following numbers in scientific notation. Use the number line from Problem #1 if it helps.

   a. 0.8   b. 0.0013   c. 0.0000972   d. 0.0000056

Questions and Conversations for #4

» *In the second row of the table, why do we write 1.7 tenths instead of 17 hundredths?* We write 0.17 as 1.7 tenths because the highest place value (order of magnitude) is in the tenths position.

» *Why do 0.000146 and 0.003772 have different place value names even though they have the same number of places to the right of the decimal?* The leftmost non-zero digit determines the order of magnitude, and this is not the same for the two numbers.

» *When you write a number in scientific notation, why is the order of magnitude of the first number always one?* This happens automatically when the power of 10 equals the order of magnitude.

Solution for #4

	Problem	Order of Magnitude Notation	Scientific Notation
a.	0.8	8 tenths	8×10^{-1}
b.	0.0013	1.3 thousandths	1.3×10^{-3}
c.	0.0000972	9.72 hundred-thousandths	9.72×10^{-5}
d.	0.0000056	5.6 millionths	5.6×10^{-6}

Find the values in Problems #5–#9 by developing your own strategies based on place value or scientific notation. Avoid using calculators or methods that involve writing out a lot of zeros. Show your work and explain why your strategies make sense.

Problem #5

5. a. 0.03×0.4 b. 0.006×2000 c. $7,000,000 \times 0.12$

Questions and Conversations for #5

» *Are there ways to separate the place value portion of the computation from calculations with the digits?* Yes, there are many ways to do this. For example, consider thinking of 0.03×0.4 as $(3 \times 0.01) \times (4 \times 0.1)$. How can you proceed from here?

» *Can it help to estimate?* Absolutely! For example, if you multiply a number by 0.4, you know that the answer will be somewhat less than half of the number.

» *If you make the first number you are multiplying 10 times as large, what must you do to the second number to keep the product the same?* You will need to make the second number one tenth as large. How might this help you simplify some calculations? How can you generalize this idea to other powers of 10 (or other numbers in general)?

» *How can scientific notation help you keep track of place value?* If you choose to write the numbers in scientific notation, the exponents on the powers of 10 can keep track of the place value for you, and the patterns you discovered in Problem #3 can help you carry out the work. Can you see how?

Solution for #5

Sample responses for a:

$$0.03 \times 0.4 = (3 \times 10^{-2}) \times (4 \times 10^{-1}) = (3 \times 4) \times (10^{-2} \times 10^{-1}) = 12 \times 10^{-3}$$

This is 12 thousandths, or 0.012. (Some may convert to scientific notation first: 1.2×10^{-2}).

Students may have many other strategies and observations. For example:

» Hundredths times tenths equals thousandths. 3×4 tells you how many thousandths.

» Add decimal places: 2 (for hundredths) + 1 (for tenths) = 3 (for thousandths).

» Use fractions: $\dfrac{3}{100} \times \dfrac{4}{10} = \dfrac{12}{1000}$. (Some students may do this intuitively even if they have not learned procedures for multiplying fractions.)

» Because 0.4 is a little less than one-half, the answer should be a little less than half of 0.03. 3 hundredths equals 30 thousandths, so half of it is 15 thousandths. 12 thousandths is a little less than this.

» Multiply the second number by 10 and compensate by dividing the first number by 10 to create the expression 0.003×4. Four groups of 3 thousandths equals 12 thousandths.

» Think of 0.4 as 0.1×4. Begin with 0.03, shift the 3 one place to the right (3 thousandths) and then multiply by 4 (12 thousandths).

Whatever strategies students use, they should be able to justify them. We will show just one approach for the other calculations, but students may use many others.

Sample response for b:
$$0.006 \times 2000 = \left(6 \times 10^{-3}\right) \times \left(2 \times 10^{3}\right) = \left(6 \times 2\right) \times \left(10^{-3} \times 10^{3}\right) = 12 \times 10^{0} = 12 \times 1 = 12$$

Sample response for c:
$$7{,}000{,}000 \times 0.12 = \left(7 \times 10^{6}\right) \times \left(1.2 \times 10^{-1}\right) = \left(7 \times 1.2\right) \times \left(10^{6} \times 10^{-1}\right) = 8.4 \times 10^{5}$$
(This is 8.4 hundred thousands, or 840,000.)

Problem #6

6. a. $40 \div 0.02$ b. $0.9 \div 30{,}000$ c. $0.00012 \div 0.04$

Questions and Conversations for #6

» *How can you tell if a quotient will be greater or less than 1?* If the dividend (the first number) is greater than the divisor (the second number), the quotient will be greater than 1. If the divisor is greater, then the quotient will be less than 1. Can you explain why?

» *How does it affect the quotient if you make the dividend 10 times as large?* It makes the quotient 10 times as large.

» *How does it affect the quotient if you make the divisor ten times as large?* It makes the quotient one tenth as large.

Teacher's Note. See Problem #5 for more ideas for conversation. Many of the same concepts apply here.

» *If you multiply the dividend by 10, what can you do to the divisor to keep the quotient the same?* You can multiply the divisor by 10 as well.

Solution for #6

Sample response for a:

$$40 \div 0.02 = \left(4 \times 10^1\right) \div \left(2 \times 10^{-2}\right) = \left(4 \div 2\right) \times \left(10^1 \div 10^{-2}\right) = 2 \times 10^3 = 2000$$

Some students may ask how many groups of 0.02 are in 40. (50 groups are in the number 1, so $40 \times 50 = 2000$ groups fit into the number 40.)

Sample response for b:

$$0.9 \div 30,000 = \left(9 \times 10^{-1}\right) \div \left(3 \times 10^4\right) = \left(9 \div 3\right) \times \left(10^{-1} \div 10^4\right) = 3 \times 10^{-5} = 0.00003$$

Sample response for c:

$$0.00012 \div 0.04 = \left(1.2 \times 10^{-4}\right) \div \left(4 \times 10^{-2}\right) = \left(1.2 \div 4\right) \times \left(10^{-4} \div 10^{-2}\right) = 0.3 \times 10^{-2}$$

This is equal to 0.003. (Some students might write the first number as 12×10^{-5}, even though this is not scientific notation. This is fine.)

Problem #7

7. If a nation's debt is about 17,000,000,000,000 dollars and the population is about 320,000,000 people, what is each person's approximate share of the debt? (These numbers are close to the figures for the U.S. at the time of this writing.)

Teacher's Note. Consider having students experiment with the effects of rounding the numbers before they calculate. They might be surprised by how much it can sometimes affect the quotient when they change the divisor by a small amount. For example, in Problem #8, if they divide 348,000 by 0.004 (instead of 0.0042), the answer increases by more than 4 million. It might help to compensate for this when rounding the dividend. The answer should also be rounded to reflect this effect.

Questions and Conversations for #7

» *Can the strategies from Problems #5 and #6 be helpful for these story problems?* Yes, all of them can help. Consider estimating, separating the place value from the values of the digits, using scientific notation, or changing the value of one number and compensating by changing the value of the other so that the answer is not affected.

» *How many digits should you show in your answer?* Consider a couple of things. First, take into account the nature of the question. How many decimal places are needed to provide a satisfactory answer to the question from a real-life perspective? Also, how precise was the given information? A rough rule of thumb is that your answer should not contain many more decimal places of precision than the numbers you used to calculate it. (Some students may be interested in doing research on how to work with *significant digits*.)

Solution for #7

Answer: a little more than $50,000

Sample solution process: Find 17,000,000,000,000 dollars ÷ 320,000,000 people. Round to 340,000,000 people because it will be easier to divide without a calculator.

$$17,000,000,000,000 \div 340,000,000 = (1.7 \times 10^{13}) \div (3.4 \times 10^8) = (1.7 \div 3.4) \times$$
$$(10^{13} \div 10^8) = 0.5 \times 10^5 = 50,000$$

The answer is more than $50,000 because you are dividing by a larger number than given, making this answer a little too small. Some students may think of 0.5×10^5 as half of 100,000. Other may use a process of compensation (multiply the first number by 10, and compensate by dividing the second number by 10) to rewrite it as 5×10^4, thereby expressing it in scientific notation.

Problem #8

8. Dollar bills are about 0.0042 inches thick and Mount Everest is about 348,000 inches tall. Approximately how many dollar bills would you stack to reach the top of Mount Everest?

Questions and Conversations for #8

See Questions and Conversations for #7.

Teacher's Notes.
- The goal is for students to develop their own strategies for computing with large and small numbers and to attend to the reasonableness of their results. Encourage them to work without calculators, at least at first.
- Challenge students to use scientific notation, at least as part of their strategy.
- Remind students to pay close attention to the units in the stories and questions they create.
- Consider having students use calculators as one means to check their results. Be ready to offer help if they have trouble entering and reading scientific notation.

Solution for #8

Answer: about 80 million dollar bills

Sample solution process: Find 348,000 inches ÷ 0.0042 inches per dollar bill. Round these numbers to 320,000 and 0.004 to make it easier to divide without a calculator.

$$320,000 \div 0.004 = \left(3.2 \times 10^5\right) \div \left(4 \times 10^{-3}\right) = \left(3.2 \div 4\right) \times \left(10^5 \div 10^{-3}\right) = 0.8 \times 10^8 =$$
$$8 \times 10^7 = 80,000,000$$

Problem #9

9. Suppose a hummingbird flaps its wings about once every 0.038 seconds. Given that light travels one mile in about 0.0000054 seconds, about how many miles will light travel in one flap of the hummingbird's wings?

Questions and Conversations for #9

See Questions and Conversations for #7.

Teacher's Note. Some students may find it more intuitive to think in terms of flaps per second (about 26) and miles per second (about 186,000). (These are the reciprocals of the original numbers.)

Solution for #9

Answer: about 7,000 miles (a little less than the diameter of the Earth!)

Sample solution process: Find 0.038 seconds per flap ÷ 0.0000054 seconds per mile. Round these numbers to 0.035 and 0.000005 to make it easier to divide without a calculator.

$$0.035 \div 0.000005 = \left(3.5 \times 10^{-2}\right) \div \left(5 \times 10^{-6}\right) = \left(3.5 \div 5\right) \times \left(10^{-2} \div 10^{-6}\right) = 0.7 \times 10^4 =$$
$$7 \times 10^3 = 7000$$

STAGE 3

Problem #10

10. Select items from the following data* to create and answer at least three story problems. Show your work or explain your strategies. You may use a calculator, but you should also apply mental math and estimation skills to insure that your results are reasonable.

distance to the nearest star beyond our solar system	4.3 light years**
average distance from the Earth to the Sun	93,000,000 miles
average distance from the Earth to the Moon	240,000 miles
diameter of the Earth	7,900 miles
diameter of a grain of sand (sample)	0.0002 meters

diameter of a red blood cell	0.000007 meters
diameter of a water molecule	0.0000000003 meters
weight of a mosquito (sample)	0.000088 ounces
weight of an African elephant (sample)	7000 pounds
mass of the Empire State Building	300,000,000 kilograms
mass of the Earth	5.97×10^{24} kilograms
one cycle of vibration for the highest note on a piano	0.00024 seconds
time interval for the blink of an eye (sample)	0.3 seconds
total lifetime of the sun	11,000,000,000 years
rate of movement of continental plates (sample)	2 centimeters per year
rate of human hair growth (sample)	0.5 inches per month
current speed of Voyager 1 spacecraft	17.1 kilometers per second
speed of sound	760 miles per hour
speed of light in a vacuum***	299,792,458 meters per second

*Some values are quite variable. These are labeled with the word "sample" and a typical value is shown. Remember that measured values are never exact.

**A light year is the distance that light travels in one year.

***This value is exact because it is a universal constant and the length of a meter is actually defined (in part) by it!

> **Teacher's Note.** If students want to collect their own "extreme" data and use it in addition to or instead of the data provided here to create their stories, encourage them to do this!

Questions and Conversations for #10

See Questions and Conversations for #7.

Solution for #10

Sample stories:

» How long will it take Voyager 1 to reach the nearest star at its present speed?

» How many times does the highest note on a piano vibrate in the blink of an eye?

Encourage students to be creative and to produce at least one question that requires multiple solution steps. (One way to do this is to write questions that require converting between units.)

WRAP UP

Share Strategies

Have students share and compare strategies for multiplying and dividing large and small numbers, and for creating and solving story problems. They should listen carefully, ask questions, and critique each other's ideas. They might be surprised that there are so many different ways to think about these calculations!

Summarize

Answer any remaining questions that students have. Summarize a few key ideas:

» When you "add zeros," "cross off zeros," or "move the decimal" to multiply or divide by powers (or multiples) of 10, you are really changing the size of a number by shifting its digits to different place values.

» The *order of magnitude* of a number is its highest place value. An advantage of using the *order of magnitude* to name a number is that it makes the approximate size of the number immediately apparent.

» *Scientific notation* is used to simplify the process of reading, writing, and calculating with very large and very small numbers. Because it is based on the order of magnitude, it also has the advantage of making the size of a number visible at a glance.

» When you calculate with decimals, you should stay focused on the sizes of the numbers and the meanings of the operations. For example, you can think of division as "how many groups of the divisor are in the dividend" or as "the size of the groups when you split the dividend into parts of equal size."

» By observing patterns in calculations, you can discover properties of exponents. You can use these properties to simplify decimal multiplication and division computations. (Many students may be able to express these patterns algebraically. For instance, the equation $10^{m} \times 10^{n} = 10^{m+n}$ shows a useful connection between multiplying exponential expressions and adding exponents.)

Further Exploration

Ask students to think of ways to continue or extend this exploration. Here are some possibilities:

» Develop and solve more real-world problems involving "extreme" numbers. Choose topics of interest to you and gather the necessary data.

» Continue practicing large and small number computation. Use multiple strategies, including ideas that you learned from other students.

EXPLORATION 8: EXTREME CALCULATIONS

» Do some research to learn what a "Fermi question" is. Look some of them up and try to answer them. Create your own Fermi questions and solve them!

» Select some data from Stage 3 and do some research to determine the range of the values (for instance, the smallest and largest weights for African elephants). Redo your calculations using both values. How strongly does this affect the answers? What implications does this have for decisions about rounding?

» Make lines like those in Problem #1 using bases other than Base Ten. Test your results with a calculator. If you have completed one or both of the Torran Math explorations, think about how the Torrans might draw a number line like this. What does all of this tell you about negative exponents?

Exploration **9**
Multiplication Slide Rules

INTRODUCTION

Materials

- » Scissors (to cut slide rule sheets into three strips) and tape
- » Rulers (to illustrate how to use addition slide rules)
- » Scientific calculators

Prior Knowledge

- » Locate and name positive numbers to the nearest thousandth on a number line.
- » Complete Stage 1 of Exploration 8: Extreme Calculations.
- » Add positive and negative integers (recommended for Stage 2).

Learning Goals

- » Locate and name negative numbers to the nearest thousandth on a number line.
- » Visualize and understand how logarithmic scales relate to multiplication.
- » Discover, describe, and extend patterns on a logarithmic scale.
- » Create and justify strategies for locating points on a logarithmic scale.
- » Connect logarithmic scales to place value, scientific notation, and exponents.
- » Communicate complex mathematical ideas clearly.
- » Persist in solving challenging problems.

Note. We use the phrase *multiplication scale* with students instead of *logarithmic scale* until we wrap up the exploration at the end.

Launching the Exploration

Motivation and purpose. To students: Before the invention of handheld calculators, slide rules were often the tool of choice. Slide rules have a variety of scales (including a special scale for multiplication) that you can slide past each other in order to perform calculations. Although slide rules themselves are rarely used any more, the multiplication scales have applications in quantifying strengths of earthquakes, loudness of sound, brightness of stars, acidity of chemicals, and frequencies in musical scales. They are also a great tool for visualizing powers of 10 and developing a deeper understanding of numerous algebraic concepts.

Understanding the Problem. Show students how to use two standard rulers as an *addition slide rule*. For example, to calculate $2+3$, align 0 on one ruler above the number 2 on the other. Trace over to 3 on the upper ruler and then drop down to see the sum, 5. Tell students that you can use the same method to multiply if you have a ruler with a specially designed scale.

On the first page of the Slide Rules handout (p. 142), have students cut along the six grey dotted lines to separate the three pairs of scales. Tell them that the top scale in each pair (the one with the 10 unequally spaced dots) is a *multiplication scale*.

The lower scale in each pair will be used as a one-unit ruler (also called an addition scale). When students are asked to show the "measurement" of a number on the multiplication scale, this means to read the number directly below it on the ruler. Students may find it helpful to see an example of this. Below is a picture of a small portion of the number lines that can be used to find the measurement for 2. The vertical bar shows that the number 2 aligns with a number slightly larger than 0.3 on the addition scale.

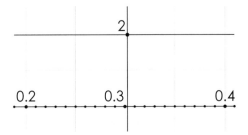

The interval between 0.3 and 0.4 is separated by dots into 10 equal parts (hundredths) which would be labeled 0.31, 0.32, 0.33, 0.34, etc. The vertical bar showing the measurement for 2 crosses the addition scale between the dots for 0.30 and 0.31. This small region can also be separated into 10 equal parts (thousandths), but these are too small to show clearly on the line. This is where students must estimate. Because the bar crosses just barely to the right of 0.30, most students will probably estimate 0.301, which is the correct measurement for 2 to the nearest thousandth. (The actual decimal goes on forever!)

STUDENT HANDOUT

Stage 1

1. Explain how to use the two numbered multiplication scales on the first page of the Slide Rules handout (see p. 142) to calculate $2 \cdot 3$. Draw a picture if it helps.

2. The scale directly below each multiplication scale is a 1-unit ruler. Use this ruler to find the measurements of 2, 3, and 6 on the multiplication scale. What is the relationship between these three measurements? Explain why this happens.

3. Explore! Find some more sets of three numbers on the scale whose measurements have the same relationship. Give at least one example and explain your thinking.

4. Extend your number line by taping an unlabeled copy of the scales to the right of one of your numbered copies. Carefully align the last mark on the first scale with the first mark on the new scale. (You will need to overlap or cut off some paper.) Label the new part of the ruler in tenths, from 1 to 2. Then figure out how to label the marks on the multiplication scale beginning at 10. Explain your thinking.

5. On the right half of your extended multiplication scale, locate and label at least five more whole numbers as precisely as you can. If you haven't done this already, use the ruler to measure each of these numbers just as you did earlier for 2, 3, and 6. Describe your thinking process. Are there some whole numbers that you wouldn't be able to locate using these methods? If so, which ones? Why?

6. Invent a procedure for using your slide rule to divide numbers without using the ruler on the bottom scale. Then find a method that does use the ruler. Describe both methods clearly with an example. What are the advantages and disadvantages of each? (Suggested example: $20 \div 5$)

7. Now that you know how to use your multiplication scale to divide, locate the mixed numbers $1\frac{1}{4}$, $1\frac{1}{2}$, and $1\frac{3}{4}$ on this scale as precisely as you can. Show the measurement of each to the nearest thousandth. Describe your methods using at least one example. Is $1\frac{1}{2}$ located exactly halfway between $1\frac{1}{4}$ and $1\frac{3}{4}$ on the multiplication scale? Explain.

8. Imagine attaching a third copy of the multiplication scale to the right of the first two. What would be the last number on the scale? Why? How many (total) copies would you need to reach the number 1 million? Explain.

9. Cut out two more pairs of scales from the second page of the Slide Rules handout (see p. 143). Tape them to the left of your extended scale. Label the dots on the multiplication scales and the rulers. Explain how you know how to label the multiplication scales.

10. How many pages to the left of the number 1 would you need in order to reach the number 0 on your multiplication scale? Explain.

11. Use the multiplication scale to explore related calculations such as $3 \cdot 2$, $3 \cdot 20$, $30 \cdot 20$, $30 \cdot 200$, $0.3 \cdot 0.2$, $0.03 \cdot 0.2$, $0.03 \cdot 200$, etc. List the ruler measurements for your numbers. Describe any observations or interesting patterns, including connections to the concepts of order of magnitude and scientific notation.

12. Explain or show how to find the number $\frac{1}{3}$ on your multiplication scale. Give its measurement to the nearest thousandth. Repeat for $\frac{2}{3}$ and 1.5. What do you observe? Why does this happen?

13. For each of the six pairs of numbers below, find the number that is exactly halfway between them on the multiplication scale. If the answer is not a whole number, give its approximate value to the nearest thousandth. The pairs are grouped into three sets. Explain your thinking for each set: How did you find the middle number? What did you observe? Why does this happen?

    a. Set 1: 1 and 10   1 and 6

    b. Set 2: 2 and 18   3 and 48

    c. Set 3: 35 and 875   6 and 42

14. Use words or an algebraic expression to show a rule that will turn a number, x, on the ruler (bottom scale) into its corresponding number, y, on the multiplication scale. Give at least three examples as evidence that your rule works. Include at least one x value that is not an integer (in other words, neither a whole number nor its opposite).

15. Use the rule you just discovered to find a new method to calculate the number halfway between two numbers on the multiplication scale. Describe your method using at least one example chosen from the pairs in Problem #13.

TEACHER'S GUIDE

STAGE 1

Problem #1

1. Explain how to use the two numbered multiplication scales on the first page of the Slide Rules handout (see p. 142) to calculate $2 \cdot 3$. Draw a picture if it helps.

Questions and Conversations for #1

This section contains ideas for conversations, mainly in the form of questions that students may ask or that you may pose to them. Be sure to allow students to do most of the thinking and talking!

 » *How can you apply what you learned about using a slide rule for addition?* Consider trying the same process. It's the scale that changes, not the procedure.

Solution for #1

Take the second copy of your multiplication scale and slide it so that the number 1 is directly above the number 2 (or 3) on your original scale. Read over to the number 3 (or 2) on the top scale and then drop directly down to the first scale. You land on the answer, the number 6!

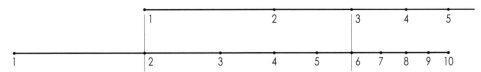

Problem #2

2. The scale directly below each multiplication scale is a 1-unit ruler. Use this ruler to find the measurements of 2, 3, and 6 on the multiplication scale. What is the relationship between these three measurements? Explain why this happens.

Questions and Conversations for #2

 » *What can you do to the first two measurements to get the third one?* Try different operations. See what happens!
 » *How does the relationship between the three numbers connect to the process you used in Problem #1?* Each measurement tells you how far you are from the number 1 on the multiplication scale. Carry out the process in Problem

#1 again, but now look for where the three measurements fit into the procedure.

» *Why does the multiplication scale start with the number 1 instead of 0?* Think about what happens when you multiply a number by 1.

Solution for #2

Answers: 0.301 units, 0.477 units, 0.778 units. The distance between 1 and 6 is the sum of the other two distances. The distances must add in this way if the slide rule is to work as described above!

Problem #3

3. Explore! Find some more sets of three numbers on the scale whose measurements have the same relationship. Give at least one example and explain your thinking.

Questions and Conversations for #3

» *What relationship between the numbers 2, 3, and 6 causes their measurements to combine in the way they do?* $2 \cdot 3 = 6$

> **Teacher's Note.** In my experience, students can usually find these measurements accurately to the nearest thousandth when they use the process described in the Introduction to this exploration. However, since they may sometimes be off by one thousandth or so, it is important to stress the fact that no measurement is ever perfect, and their numbers may not always appear to add exactly.

Solution for #3

Other sets of three numbers include: 1, 7, and 7; 2, 2, and 4; 2, 4, and 8; 2, 5, and 10; 3, 3, and 9. The largest number should always be the product of the other two.

Example: The measurements for 2, 4, and 8 are 0.301, 0.602, and 0.903 units. The distance between 1 and 8 is the sum of the other two distances.

Problem #4

4. Extend your number line by taping an unlabeled copy of the scales to the right of one of your numbered copies. Carefully align the last mark on the first scale with the first mark on the new scale. (You will need to overlap or cut off some paper.) Label the new part of the ruler in tenths, from 1 to 2. Then figure out how to label the marks on the multiplication scale beginning at 10. Explain your thinking.

Questions and Conversations for #4

» *What happens to numbers on the multiplication scale as you move to the right?* The numbers seem to get more closely spaced.

» *Why is the last number on the new multiplication scale not 20?* This is partly due to the answer to the previous question. Also, the multiplication slide rule will not work if you choose 20 as the last number.

Solution for #4

See the Solution to #5 for a picture of how to label the dots on the new scales. The new marks on the multiplication scale are multiples of 10 because each number on the second page is 10 times as large as the number at the corresponding mark on the first page. According to our slide rule procedure, this means it must be 1 unit to the right of it. For example, because 2 is located above 0.301 on the first page, 20 must be located above 1.301 on the second page.

Problem #5

5. On the right half of your extended multiplication scale, locate and label at least five more whole numbers as precisely as you can. If you haven't done this already, use the ruler to measure each of these numbers just as you did earlier for 2, 3, and 6. Describe your thinking process. Are there some whole numbers that you wouldn't be able to locate using these methods? If so, which ones? Why?

Questions and Conversations for #5

» *You've seen two methods for locating new numbers on the multiplication scale. What are they?* One method is to use the slide rule (physically line up the numbers, count over and drop down). The other approach involves adding the measurements of the two factors.

» *One number you probably cannot find using your current methods is 11. What is another example? Why?* Another example is 13. Think of whole numbers that have products of 11 or 13.

Solution for #5

Sample values of 12, 14, 15, 16, and 18 are shown. The measurements for these five numbers are: 1.079, 1.146, 1.176, 1.204, and 1.255 units respectively.

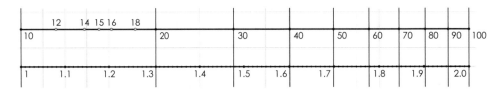

You can locate the numbers by finding a whole number multiplication equation and then physically using the slide rule. To locate the numbers more precisely, you can add the corresponding measurements on the ruler. For example, because $12 = 3 \cdot 4$, you can add the measurements for 3 (0.477 units) and 4 (0.602 units) to get the measurement for 12 (1.079 units).

You can't use these methods to locate any number that has a prime factor greater than 10 because you will not be able to create a multiplication expression for which you know the measurement of each factor. (Later, students may discover other ways to locate these numbers.)

> **Teacher's Note.** You can use the "log" key on a scientific calculator to check students' work quickly when they choose numbers greater than 20. For example, the measurement for 35 is $\log(35) \approx 1.544$.

STAGE 2

Problem #6

6. Invent a procedure for using your slide rule to divide numbers without using the ruler on the bottom scale. Then find a method that does use the ruler. Describe both methods clearly with an example. What are the advantages and disadvantages of each? (Suggested example: $20 \div 5$)

Questions and Conversations for #6

   » *How can your knowledge of multiplication help you devise a procedure for division?* Think backward!

Solution for #6

We'll use $20 \div 5$ as our example. To do it without using the ruler, align 5 on the upper multiplication scale with 20 on the lower one. Find the number 1 on the upper scale and drop straight down to the lower one. You will land on the quotient, 4!

To use the ruler, subtract the measurement of 5 (0.699) from that of 20 (1.301) to get 0.602, which is the measurement for the number 4. The first method is more visual and intuitive for many people. The second method is generally more precise.

Problem #7

7. Now that you know how to use your multiplication scale to divide, locate the mixed numbers $1\frac{1}{4}$, $1\frac{1}{2}$, and $1\frac{3}{4}$ on this scale as precisely as you can. Show the measurement of each to the nearest thousandth. Describe your methods using at least one example. Is $1\frac{1}{2}$ located exactly halfway between $1\frac{1}{4}$ and $1\frac{3}{4}$ on the multiplication scale? Explain.

Questions and Conversations for #7

» *By what could you multiply each mixed number to turn it into a whole number?* If you're not sure, try adding the mixed number to itself repeatedly.

» *What method helps you locate numbers more precisely on the multiplication scale?* Adding the measurements from the ruler is generally more accurate than using the slide rule physically.

» *How can you know if numbers are equally spaced on the multiplication scale when it's hard to tell visually?* Again, it can help to use the measurements.

Solution for #7

You can find the numbers $1\frac{1}{4}$, $1\frac{1}{2}$, and $1\frac{3}{4}$ by using the expressions $5 \div 4$, $3 \div 2$, and $7 \div 4$ respectively. Because you're asked to be as precise as possible, it's probably better to subtract the measurements than to physically slide the scales.

$$1\frac{1}{4} \qquad 0.699 - 0.602 = 0.097 \text{ units}$$

$$1\frac{1}{2} \qquad 0.477 - 0.301 = 0.176 \text{ units}$$

$$1\frac{3}{4} \qquad 0.845 - 0.602 = 0.243 \text{ units}$$

These numbers are not equally spaced. $1\frac{1}{4}$ and $1\frac{1}{2}$ are $0.176 - 0.097 = 0.079$ units apart, while $1\frac{1}{2}$ and $1\frac{3}{4}$ are $0.243 - 0.176 = 0.067$ units apart. Also, $1\frac{1}{2}$ is not exactly halfway between 1 and 2. The halfway mark is at about $0.301 \div 2 = 0.1505$ units on the ruler, while $1\frac{1}{2}$ is located at 0.176 units. This is not surprising because numbers get closer together on the multiplication scale as they become larger.

Problem #8

8. Imagine attaching a third copy of the multiplication scale to the right of the first two. What would be the last number on the scale? Why? How many (total) copies would you need to reach the number 1 million? Explain.

Questions and Conversations for #8

» *Do you see any patterns developing with the multiplication scale numbers at the beginning and end of each page?* There is a pattern involving repeated multiplication.

Solution for #8

The last number on the third page of the multiplication scale is 1000 because the final number on each successive page is 10 times as large. This happens because a shift of 1 unit to the right on the ruler always corresponds to multiplication by 10.

You will need 6 pages to reach the number 1 million, because $10^6 = 1,000,000$.

Problem #9

9. Cut out two more pairs of scales from the second page of the Slide Rules handout (see p. 143). Tape them to the left of your extended scale. Label the dots on the multiplication scales and the rulers. Explain how you know how to label the multiplication scales.

Questions and Conversations for #9

» *How can you continue the pattern from Problem #8 in the opposite direction?* This is another opportunity to think backward!

Teacher's Note. Don't be surprised if some students have more trouble labeling the ruler than the multiplication scale! They might be unaccustomed to visualizing negative decimals. Encourage them to view the ruler as a number line.

Solution for #9

The two parts of the scales look like this:

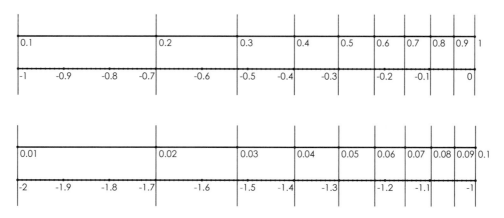

To find the numbers on the multiplication scale, divide each corresponding number on the page to the right of it by 10. To find the numbers on the ruler, just keep counting backward by tenths as you move to the left.

Problem #10

10. How many pages to the left of the number 1 would you need in order to reach the number 0 on your multiplication scale? Explain.

Questions and Conversations for #10

» *Is this a "trick question"?* It's not meant to trick you—just to make you think carefully. The answer is a little strange, though!

Solution for #10

You will never reach the number 0 on the multiplication scale no matter how many pages you use! As you keep dividing by 10, the values get closer and closer to 0, but never reach it.

Problem #11

11. Use the multiplication scale to explore related calculations such as $3 \cdot 2$, $3 \cdot 20$, $30 \cdot 20$, $30 \cdot 200$, $0.3 \cdot 0.2$, $0.03 \cdot 0.2$, $0.03 \cdot 200$, etc. List the ruler measurements for your numbers. Describe any observations or interesting patterns, including connections to the concepts of order of magnitude and scientific notation.

Questions and Conversations for #11

» *What kinds of information should you collect? How should you organize it?* It would help to write equations in both standard and scientific notations, and to compare these with equations based on the ruler measurements. You might make a table to organize the information.

» *What happens on the multiplication scale when you change the place value of a digit?* The number moves to the corresponding location on another "page" of the scale.

Solution for #11

Sample student response:

To highlight connections, we will collect and organize information about scientific notation and the ruler measurements.

Equation	Scientific Notation	Ruler Measurements
$3 \cdot 2 = 6$	$(3 \times 10^0) \times (2 \times 10^0) = 6 \times 10^0$	$0.477 + 0.301 = 0.778$
$3 \cdot 20 = 60$	$(3 \times 10^0) \times (2 \times 10^1) = 6 \times 10^1$	$0.477 + 1.301 = 1.778$
$30 \cdot 20 = 600$	$(3 \times 10^1) \times (2 \times 10^1) = 6 \times 10^2$	$1.477 + 1.301 = 2.778$
$30 \cdot 200 = 6000$	$(3 \times 10^1) \times (2 \times 10^2) = 6 \times 10^3$	$1.477 + 2.301 = 3.778$
$0.3 \cdot 0.2 = 0.06$	$(3 \times 10^{-1}) \times (2 \times 10^{-1}) = 6 \times 10^{-2}$	$-0.523 + -0.699 = -1.222$
$0.03 \cdot 0.2 = 0.006$	$(3 \times 10^{-2}) \times (2 \times 10^{-1}) = 6 \times 10^{-3}$	$-1.523 + -0.699 = -2.222$
$0.03 \cdot 200 = 6$	$(3 \times 10^{-2}) \times (2 \times 10^2) = 6 \times 10^0$	$-1.523 + 2.301 = 0.778$

Sample observations:

» Each "page" of the multiplication scale represents an order of magnitude. The first page is the ones place, the next to the right is the tens, etc.

» The decimal portion of the measurement for a given digit is the same for all numbers greater than or equal to 1. It has a different value for numbers less than 1.

» The ruler measurement "rounded down" to the nearest integer (the *greatest integer* of the measurement) is equal to the exponent in scientific notation. Both represent the order of magnitude of the number.

» Adding the exponents in the scientific notation equations corresponds to adding the *greatest integers* of the measurements. (For numbers greater than one, this is just the whole number part of the measurement.)

STAGE 3

Problem #12

12. Explain or show how to find the number $\frac{1}{3}$ on your multiplication scale. Give its measurement to the nearest thousandth. Repeat for $\frac{2}{3}$ and 1.5. What do you observe? Why does this happen?

Questions and Conversations for #12

» *Can it help to make a connection with an earlier question?* Problem #7 also involves fractions. Think about what you did there.

» *Does the measurement for $\frac{1}{3}$ remind you of any other measurements?* It should look similar to the measurement for 3. Is this a coincidence?

Solution for #12

One way to locate each number is to write its value as a division expression and subtract the corresponding measurements.

$$\frac{1}{3} = 1 \div 3 \qquad 0 - 0.477 = -0.477 \text{ units}$$

$$\frac{2}{3} = 2 \div 3 \qquad 0.301 - 0.477 = -0.176 \text{ units}$$

$$1.5 = 3 \div 2 \qquad 0.477 - 0.301 = 0.176 \text{ units}$$

The measurements of $\frac{2}{3}$ and 1.5 are opposites. Some students might recognize that $\frac{1}{3}$ and 3 also have opposite measurements. In general, this will happen with any pair of numbers that has a product of 1 (i.e., any reciprocal pair). This makes

151

sense because the number 1 on the multiplication scale is located at 0 on the ruler, and if the sum of two numbers is 0, they are opposites.

Problem #13

13. For each of the six pairs of numbers below, find the number that is exactly halfway between them on the multiplication scale. If the answer is not a whole number, give its approximate value to the nearest thousandth. The pairs are grouped into three sets. Explain your thinking for each set: How did you find the middle number? What did you observe? Why does this happen?
    a. Set 1:   1 and 10   1 and 6
    b. Set 2:   2 and 18   3 and 48
    c. Set 3:   35 and 875   6 and 42

Questions and Conversations for #13

» *Can you think of pairs for which it would be easier to find the "middle" number? Consider perfect squares. What is halfway between 1 and 9? 1 and 100? Why?*

» *What happens when you jump equal distances on the multiplication scale?* You are multiplying by the same number each time.

Solution for #13

Set 1:   1 and 10: $\sqrt{10} \approx 3.162$ 1 and 6: $\sqrt{6} \approx 2.449$
Set 2:   2 and 18: 6   3 and 48: 12
Set 3:   35 and 875: 175   6 and 42: $6 \cdot \sqrt{7} = \sqrt{252} \approx 15.875$

Set 1: The number halfway between 1 and a given number, n, on the multiplication scale is the square root of n. To see why, start at 0 on the ruler, jump halfway, and then the rest of the way to the number directly below n. On the multiplication scale, this corresponds to starting at 1 and multiplying by the same number twice to get to n. That number is the square root!

Set 2: Now you're starting at numbers different than 1, but the basic idea is the same. You can experiment to find that $2 \cdot 3 = 6$ and $6 \cdot 3 = 18$. You are jumping from 2 to 6 to 18, multiplying by 3 each time, so 6 is the number in the middle. For the second pair of numbers, $3 \cdot 4 = 12$ and $12 \cdot 4 = 48$, so 12 is the middle number.

Some students may discover a strategy that does not require trial and error. Divide the two numbers, take the square root of the result and multiply this by the smaller number. For example, to find the number halfway between 2 and 18:

$$18 \div 2 = 9 \qquad\qquad \sqrt{9} = 3 \qquad\qquad 2 \cdot 3 = 6$$

Set 3: If you apply this strategy to the final two pairs, you will get:

$$875 \div 35 = 25 \qquad \sqrt{25} = 5 \qquad 35 \cdot 5 = 175$$

$$42 \div 6 = 7 \qquad \sqrt{7} \approx 2.6458 \qquad 6 \cdot \sqrt{7} \approx 6 \cdot 2.6458 \approx 15.875$$

Problem #14

14. Use words or an algebraic expression to show a rule that will turn a number, x, on the ruler (bottom scale) into its corresponding number, y, on the multiplication scale. Give at least three examples as evidence that your rule works. Include at least one x value that is not an integer (in other words, neither a whole number nor its opposite).

> **Teacher's Note.** You can express this process algebraically as $a \cdot \sqrt{\dfrac{b}{a}}$. A few students may even discover that you can write it more simply as $\sqrt{a \cdot b}$. (This middle value on the multiplication scale is called the *geometric mean* of a and b.)

Questions and Conversations for #14

» *Which are the easiest numbers on your ruler (x values) to focus on?* The whole numbers are probably the easiest. The negative integers are probably next. Decimal values between these are more difficult.

» *How can you make use of patterns that you have already discovered?* Patterns can generally be described using formulas or words. Look for ways that the patterns involve connections between the x and the y values.

Solution for #14

By focusing on simpler numbers such as those at the beginning and end of each page, you can create a table to see what the rule must do.

x	-2	-1	0	1	2
y	0.01	0.1	1	10	100

This suggests the rule $y = 10^x$. It works for the numbers in the table (for example, $10^2 = 100$ and $10^{-1} = 0.1$) but does it work for others as well? You can use your calculator to find that $10^{0.301} \approx 2$ and $10^{0.477} \approx 3$. Because these exponents are the measurements for the numbers 2 and 3, this supports the conclusion.

> **Teacher's Note.** By making a connection to the previous question, some students may conjecture (correctly) that an exponent of 0.5 represents a square root!

Problem #15

15. Use the rule you just discovered to find a new method to calculate the number halfway between two numbers on the multiplication scale. Describe your method using at least one example chosen from the pairs in Problem #13.

Questions and Conversations for #15

» *How can you calculate the number exactly in the middle of two numbers on the ruler?* There are many ways. For example, you might think about how to use the distance between the two numbers. You also know an "equal sharing" process that might be helpful. (This is the mean or average.)

» *If you know a "middle number" on the ruler, can it help you find a corresponding middle number on the multiplication scale?* Yes. Your answer to Problem #14 can help you make the connection.

Solution for #15

The measurements for 2 and 18 are approximately 0.301 and 1.255 units. One way to find the middle number between these is to calculate the mean:

$$(0.301 + 1.255) \div 2 = 0.778$$

Now use the rule $y = 10^x$ to find the number corresponding with 0.778 on the multiplication scale: $10^{0.778} \approx 6$, the same answer as before!

WRAP UP

Share Strategies

Have students share and compare strategies. If they completed Problem #14, ask them how they might use the their rule to locate the number 11 on the multiplication scale. (They could take 10 to various powers until they get a result as close as possible to 11. The answer is approximately 1.041)

Summarize

Answer any remaining questions that students have. Summarize a few key points and share some new information:

» If students have done the first question from Exploration 8: Extreme Calculations, look at how the multiplication scale essentially fills in the numbers between the powers of 10 in a way that preserves and extends the existing patterns of multiplication!

» Ask students how they might reverse the process from Problem #14 to turn a number y on the multiplication scale into the corresponding number x on the ruler. They might guess some type of "root" involving the number 10. Point out that although this could work for x^{10}, it does not make sense for the expression 10^x.

» Tell students that the real mathematical name for a multiplication scale is a *logarithmic scale*. Have students experiment with the "log" key on their calculator. They should discover that $\log(1) = 0$, $\log(100) = 2$, $\log(2) \approx 0.301$, etc. The input is the number on the logarithmic scale and the output is the corresponding measurement on the ruler! Therefore, the logarithm of a number is the exponent on a base of 10 that will produce that number.

Further Exploration

Ask students to think of ways to continue or extend this exploration. Here are some possibilities:

» Read about when and how logarithms were invented and used to simplify calculations.

» Research real-life uses of logarithmic scales including the *decibel scale* (sound), the *Richter scale* (earthquakes), the *pH scale* (chemistry), the stellar magnitude scale (astronomy), and frequencies in musical scales.

» Explore properties of logarithms. For example, you can write the equation in Problem #2 ($0.301 + 0.477 = 0.778$) more precisely as $\log(2) + \log(3) = \log(6)$. What is the pattern, and how can you express it, and similar ones, algebraically? Think about how these patterns relate to properties of exponents. Partial answer: $\log(a) + \log(b) = \log(a \cdot b)$

» If you are familiar with identities, opposites, and reciprocals, compare their locations on the ruler and the multiplication scale. Visualize and describe a connection between rules for subtraction (adding the opposite) and division (multiplying by the reciprocal).

» Read about geometric and arithmetic means. Relate them to this activity.

» If you know about cube roots, think about how you could use logarithmic scales to find them.

» If the Torrans (see Exploration 2: Torran Math) were to create a logarithmic scale with a ruler below it, what might they do differently than we do? How would this affect the values of their logarithms? How could you convert between the two systems?

Exploration 10

Factor Blocks and Radicals

INTRODUCTION

Prior Knowledge

- » Complete Stage 1 of Exploration 1: Building Blocks in the *Factors and Multiples* book, or study the appendix at the end of this book.
- » Understand the meanings of square roots and whole number exponents.

Learning Goals

- » Make connections between radicals and exponents by analyzing visual models.
- » Discover and justify properties of exponents by analyzing visual models.
- » Create strategies to generate equivalent expressions with exponents and radicals.
- » Understand the distinction between exact and approximate forms for radicals.
- » Communicate complex mathematical ideas clearly.
- » Persist in solving challenging problems.

Launching the Exploration

Motivation and purpose. To students: In this activity, you extend your understanding of exponents and radicals (roots) by following up on an idea from Exploration 1 in the *Factors and Multiples* book. By manipulating blocks that represent prime numbers, you discover important definitions and properties, some of which might surprise you. As you apply this knowledge to create multiple equivalent expressions for numbers, you will be laying a foundation for much of your future work in algebra.

Understanding the problem. If students have not done the "Building Blocks" exploration from the *Factors and Multiples* book, discuss the concepts in the appendix of this book. There are two key facts that students need to keep in mind throughout this activity:

- » Joining blocks represents multiplication.
- » Exponents count blocks (factors).

Introduce the term *radical* to students. It applies to the "$\sqrt{}$" symbol. Although students are familiar with square roots, there are other types of radicals as well.

Explain that $\sqrt{2}$ is an example of an *exact* form for a radical, while 1.4142136 is an *approximate* form. Mathematicians sometimes leave radicals in an exact form because they can be easier to work with and you can calculate any desired number of decimal places from them.

As students begin the first two or three questions, check that they understand how to use the blocks to represent prime factorizations. All prime factorizations in this exploration should be written in exponential form.

Teacher's Note. The brief discussion of radicals in this introduction might give some things away to students. They might also get hints by looking ahead at later questions in the activity as they work. This is all okay, but you don't have to go out of your way to point these things out to them!

STUDENT HANDOUT

Note. Please write all prime factorizations in exponential form.

Stage 1

1. Show block diagrams and prime factorizations for 25, 63, and 360. Then, square each number and show the answers in the same two forms.

2. Show block diagrams and prime factorizations for 25, 64, and 144. Then, find the square root of each number and show the answers in the same two forms.

3. What happened to the exponents when you squared the numbers? What happened to them when you took the square root? Can you recognize a perfect square just by looking at its block diagram or its prime factorization?

4. What happens to the value of a block if you "cut it in half"? Why? How would you write this value in exponential form? Explain using a 7 block as an example.

5. Imagine joining a 3 and a 2 block and then cutting the entire diagram in half. What number does this represent? Do you think it changes the value if you cut each block first before joining? Why or why not? Include block diagrams along with exact mathematical expressions to represent the processes of "joining" and "cutting."

6. Repeat the process in Problem #5 using a different pair of blocks. What general conjecture(s) might you make about this process? (Suggested example: a 5 and a 7 block.)

7. Draw block diagrams for $\sqrt{45}$, $\sqrt{48}$, and $\sqrt{90}$. Use them to rewrite each expression in *simplified* form (with a smaller number under the radical).

Stage 2

8. Draw block diagrams for both numbers in each pair. Then write the second number in each pair in a simpler exponential form.

   a. 5^2 and $\left(5^2\right)^3$

   b. 2^4 and $\left(2^4\right)^{\frac{1}{2}}$

   c. $3^{\frac{1}{2}}$ and $\left(3^{\frac{1}{2}}\right)^4$

9. Make a conjecture about what happens when you have a "power of a power." Explain your thinking.

10. For each block diagram, write at least five equivalent expressions that it could represent. Make use of both exponents and radicals in your examples.

    a. 3 | 7 | 11

    b. 7 | 7

    c. 2 | 2 | 2 | 11

Stage 3

11. Explore the meaning of "a third of a block." What do you think it represents? Why? Explain using at least one example.

12. Draw a block diagram for the calculation $13^{\frac{1}{2}} \cdot 13^{\frac{1}{3}}$. Use it to write the answer in three forms: (1) a single exponential expression with a base of 13, (2) a single radical, and (3) a decimal approximation.

TEACHER'S GUIDE

Note. Students should write all prime factorizations in exponential form.

STAGE 1

Problem #1

1. Show block diagrams and prime factorizations for 25, 63, and 360. Then, square each number and show the answers in the same two forms.

Questions and Conversations for #1

This section contains ideas for conversations, mainly in the form of questions that students may ask or that you may pose to them. Be sure to allow students to do most of the thinking and talking!

» *Is it possible to write an exponent for every base in a prime factorization?* Yes. If a prime factor occurs only once, you can give it an exponent of 1. This might help you recognize and describe patterns more easily.

Solution for #1

Note. The arrangement of the blocks within the diagrams does not matter.

The original numbers:

25	63	360
$\boxed{5\,|\,5}$ 5^2	$\boxed{3\,|\,3\,|\,7}$ $3^2 \cdot 7^1$	$\boxed{2\,|\,2\,|\,2\,|\,3\,|\,3\,|\,5}$ $2^3 \cdot 3^2 \cdot 5^1$

The squared numbers:

625	3969	129,600
$\boxed{\begin{array}{cc} 5 & 5 \\ 5 & 5 \end{array}}$ 5^4	$\boxed{\begin{array}{ccc} 3 & 3 & 7 \\ 3 & 3 & 7 \end{array}}$ $3^4 \cdot 7^2$	$\boxed{\begin{array}{cccccc} 2 & 2 & 2 & 3 & 3 & 5 \\ 2 & 2 & 2 & 3 & 3 & 5 \end{array}}$ $2^6 \cdot 3^4 \cdot 5^2$

Problem #2

2. Show block diagrams and prime factorizations for 25, 64, and 144. Then, find the square root of each number and show the answers in the same two forms.

Questions and Conversations for #2

See Questions and Conversations for #1.

Solution for #2

The original numbers:

25	64	144

$\boxed{5|5}$ 5^2 $\qquad$ $\boxed{2|2|2|2|2|2}$ 2^6 $\qquad$ $\boxed{2|2|2|2|3|3}$ $2^4 \cdot 3^2$

The square roots:

5	8	12

$\boxed{5}$ 5^1 $\qquad$ $\boxed{2|2|2}$ 2^3 $\qquad$ $\boxed{2|2|3}$ $2^2 \cdot 3^1$

Problem #3

3. What happened to the exponents when you squared the numbers? What happened to them when you took the square root? Can you recognize a perfect square just by looking at its block diagram or its prime factorization?

Questions and Conversations for #3

» *What is the relationship between squares and square roots?* They are inverse operations. They "undo" each other.

Solution for #3

When you square a number, each exponent in its prime factorization doubles. When you take the square root of a number, each exponent in its prime factorization becomes half a large.

The block diagram of a perfect square has an even number of blocks for each prime factor. The exponents in its prime factorization are all even numbers.

Problem #4

4. What happens to the value of a block if you "cut it in half"? Why? How would you write this value in exponential form? Explain using a 7 block as an example.

Questions and Conversations for #4

» *Why does each piece not represent the number 3.5?* Although it's true that $3.5 + 3.5 = 7$, joining blocks does not represent addition. What does it represent?
» *What number should you use as the base in your exponential expression?* Use 7 for the base.
» *How would you write the number 7 in exponential form using this base? What happens to the exponent when you cut the block in half?* You would write 7 as 7^1. The exponent becomes half as large.

> » *What do exponents tell you about the block diagrams?* They tell you how many blocks (or partial blocks!) of the base you have.
> » *How can you check that your exponential expression equals the value you found at the beginning of the question?* Try using your calculator!

Solution for #4

Think about what happens if you imagine putting the two halves back together again.

$$\boxed{7} \rightarrow \leftarrow \boxed{7}$$

Joining blocks stands for multiplying the numbers, and if you join the half-blocks you get 7. The half-blocks do not have a value of 3.5 because joining them would mean $3.5 \cdot 3.5$, which equals 12.25, not 7! Instead, you want a number that you can multiply by itself to equal 7. This is the square root of 7 ($\sqrt{7}$).

Because you have half of a 7 block, the exponential form is $7^{\frac{1}{2}}$. Students may also reason that you begin with one 7 block and that taking the square root makes the exponent half as large.

Problem #5

5. Imagine joining a 3 and a 2 block and then cutting the entire diagram in half. What number does this represent? Do you think it changes the value if you cut each block first before joining? Why or why not? Include block diagrams along with exact mathematical expressions to represent the processes of "joining" and "cutting."

> **Teacher's Note.** Students can use a calculator to verify that $\sqrt{7}$ and $7^{\frac{1}{2}}$ appear to be equal. (The approximate value is 2.64575131106.) Some may make the conjecture that a power of $\frac{1}{2}$ represents a square root in general.)

Questions and Conversations for #5

> » *What is the main difference between this question and the previous one?* Now you are joining two blocks before cutting them in half.
> » *What is the value of the block diagram if you rejoin the two halves? What does this tell you about the value of each of the two halves?* If you rejoin the two halves, the value is 6. Revisit the previous question to help you think about what the value of each half should be.
> » *If you reverse the order and cut each block in half before joining them, is the resulting block diagram the same as before? What does this suggest about its value?* Yes, it looks the same as before, so it should probably represent the same value.

» *Can you use the ideas in this question to write an equation that shows two equivalent radical expressions? How about two equivalent exponential expressions?* Yes, you can do both. Think about the order in which you do the operations.

Solution for #5

$$\boxed{2 \mid 3}$$

This diagram stands for the square root of 6 because if you join a copy of it to itself, your get the block diagram for 6 (a whole 2 block joined to a whole 3 block).

When you join the blocks, you are multiplying 2 by 3. Cutting this into two identical parts stands for taking the square root. You can represent this process as $\sqrt{2 \cdot 3}$ (or $(2 \cdot 3)^{\frac{1}{2}}$) to show that you multiply before taking the square root.

If you cut the 2 and 3 blocks first, you get the square roots: $\sqrt{2}$ and $\sqrt{3}$. When you join them, you multiply: $\sqrt{2} \cdot \sqrt{3}$. Because the resulting block diagram looks the same in either case, you might suspect that the two expressions are equal ($\sqrt{2} \cdot \sqrt{3} = \sqrt{6}$ or $2^{\frac{1}{2}} \cdot 3^{\frac{1}{2}} = (2 \cdot 3)^{\frac{1}{2}}$). Testing this on a calculator seems to support the conclusion. Each expression has an approximate value of 2.44948974278.

Problem #6

6. Repeat the process in Problem #5 using a different pair of blocks. What general conjecture(s) might you make about this process? (Suggested example: a 5 and a 7 block.)

Questions and Conversations for #6

» *Can you write your conjectures as algebraic equations?* If your conjectures relate to your equations in Problem #5, then the answer is yes.

Solution for #6

If you use a 5 and a 7 block, you get a block diagram for $\sqrt{35}$:

$$\boxed{5 \mid 7}$$

If you "join, then cut," you get $\sqrt{5 \cdot 7}$. If you "cut, then join," you get $\sqrt{5} \cdot \sqrt{7}$. Either way, you get the same block diagram, suggesting that both expressions are equal. Entering them into a calculator appears to verify this. They both have a value of approximately 5.9160797831.

The results of Problems #5 and #6 suggest the conjecture that $\sqrt{a \cdot b} = \sqrt{a} \cdot \sqrt{b}$, at least when a and b are prime numbers. In fact, this is true for any non-negative values of a and b. (How could you test this for composite numbers?)

Problem #7

7. Draw block diagrams for $\sqrt{45}$, $\sqrt{48}$, and $\sqrt{90}$. Use them to rewrite each expression in *simplified* form (with a smaller number under the radical).

Questions and Conversations for #7

» *Once you have built the block diagram for the number under the radical, how do you form the diagram for the square root?* Break the diagram into two identical pieces. Once you've done this, can you see how to write the exact value for each piece?

» *How can you find evidence that your simplified radical expression is equivalent to the one you were given?* Enter both expressions into your calculator.

» *If your calculator shows the same decimal for both radical expressions, does this prove that the two values are equal? Explain.* No, because there is the possibility that the decimals differ at some later point. However, it does provide pretty strong evidence!

Solution for #7

Build the number underneath the radical sign and then take the square root by cutting it into two identical parts (keeping just one of them). Interpret the resulting block diagram in order to create an exact expression in simplified form.

Block Diagram for 45	Block Diagram for $\sqrt{45}$	Simplified Form
3 3 5	3 5	$3 \cdot \sqrt{5}$

Note. Both $\sqrt{45}$ and $3 \cdot \sqrt{5}$ have decimal approximations of 6.7082039325.

Block Diagram for 48	Block Diagram for $\sqrt{48}$	Simplified Form
2 2 2 2 3	2 2 3	$4 \cdot \sqrt{3}$

Note. Both $\sqrt{48}$ and $4 \cdot \sqrt{3}$ have decimal approximations of 6.92820323028.

Block Diagram for 90	Block Diagram for $\sqrt{90}$	Simplified Form
2 3 3 5	2 3 5	$3 \cdot \sqrt{10}$

Note. Both $\sqrt{90}$ and $3 \cdot \sqrt{10}$ have decimal approximations of 9.48683298051

STAGE 2

Problem #8

8. Draw block diagrams for both numbers in each pair. Then write the second number in each pair in a simpler exponential form.

   a. 5^2 and $\left(5^2\right)^3$ b. 2^4 and $\left(2^4\right)^{\frac{1}{2}}$ c. $3^{\frac{1}{2}}$ and $\left(3^{\frac{1}{2}}\right)^4$

Solution for #8

a. $\boxed{5\,5}$ 5^2 $\boxed{\begin{array}{cc}5&5\\5&5\\5&5\end{array}}$ $(5^2)^3=5^6$ b. $\boxed{\begin{array}{cc}2&2\\2&2\end{array}}$ 2^4 $\boxed{\begin{array}{c}2\\2\end{array}}$ $(2^4)^{\frac{1}{2}}=2^2$ c. $\boxed{3}$ $3^{\frac{1}{2}}$ $\boxed{\begin{array}{c}3\\3\end{array}}$ $(3^{\frac{1}{2}})^4=3^2$

Problem #9

9. Make a conjecture about what happens when you have a "power of a power." Explain your thinking.

Questions and Conversations for #9

» *Can you express your conjecture algebraically?* Try beginning with $\left(a^m\right)^n$ on one side of an equation. Can you write another expression that will always produce the same result?

» *How can you test your conjecture?* Try it with a variety of values for the base and the exponents.

Solution for #9

It looks as if, when you have a "power of a power," you multiply the exponents, leaving the base the same. Think of powers as counting the number of blocks (factors) of the base, even when you extend the idea to include fractional powers. You can express this conjecture algebraically as $\left(a^m\right)^n = a^{m \cdot n}$.

Problem #10

10. For each block diagram, write at least five equivalent expressions that it could represent. Make use of both exponents and radicals in your examples.

    a. $\boxed{3\;7\;11}$ b. $\boxed{7\;7}$ c. $\boxed{2\;2\;2\;11}$

Questions and Conversations for #10

» *Can your expression contain decimal or fractional exponents? Can an exponent be a fraction other than $\dfrac{1}{2}$? Is it possible to create an expression that consists of just a single number under a radical symbol? Is it okay for a single expression to* *contain both radical signs and exponents? Can you use decimal approximations? Can you group factors together in different ways? Yes—you can do all of these things and more. Be creative!*

Solution for #10

A few of the countless possibilities for each are shown. (Students are asked to show only five of each.) Decimal values are approximate.

» *Sample response for a:* $\sqrt{693}$, $3 \cdot \sqrt{7} \cdot \sqrt{11}$, $3 \cdot 77^{\frac{1}{2}}$, $693^{\frac{1}{2}}$, $3 \cdot 7^{\frac{1}{2}} \cdot 11^{\frac{1}{2}}$, $\left(693^2\right)^{\frac{1}{4}}$, $(480,249)^{\frac{1}{4}}$, $\sqrt{63} \cdot \sqrt{11}$, $7^{0.5} \cdot 99^{0.5}$, 26.324893, etc.

» *Sample response for b:* $7 \cdot \sqrt{7}$, $\sqrt{343}$, $7 \cdot 7^{\frac{1}{2}}$, $343^{0.5}$, $7^{\frac{3}{2}}$, $7 \cdot \sqrt{\sqrt{49}}$, $\left(7^{\frac{1}{2}}\right)^3$, $\left(7^3\right)^{0.5}$, $49^{\frac{1}{2}} \cdot 7^{\frac{1}{2}}$, $(117,649)^{\frac{1}{4}}$, $7^{1.5}$, 18.520259, etc.

» *Sample response for c:* $4 \cdot \sqrt{22}$, $\sqrt{32} \cdot \sqrt{11}$, $\sqrt{352}$, $2^{2.5} \cdot 11^{0.5}$, $4 \cdot 22^{\frac{1}{2}}$, $2 \cdot 2 \cdot 2^{\frac{1}{2}} \cdot 11^{\frac{1}{2}}$, $\sqrt{16} \cdot \sqrt{2} \cdot \sqrt{11}$, $(123,904)^{0.25}$, $\left(2^5\right)^{\frac{1}{2}} \cdot \left(11^2\right)^{\frac{1}{4}}$, $\left(2^5 \cdot 11\right)^{\frac{1}{2}}$, 18.761663, etc.

STAGE 3

Problem #11

11. Explore the meaning of "a third of a block." What do you think it represents? Why? Explain using at least one example.

Questions and Conversations for #11

» *Once you have a conjecture about the meaning of a "third of a block," how can you test your idea?* Consider thinking about your idea in terms of both exponents and radicals. Use your calculator.

» *How can you use your calculator to approximate this value?* You can use the calculator's exponent key. Scientific calculators also often have a key for entering radicals other than square roots. You may have to experiment or look this up in your calculator's manual.

> **Teacher's Note for #11.** Once students have discovered the idea of "multiplying a number by itself three times," you might need to give them a name (*cube root*) and symbol ($\sqrt[3]{\ }$) for this concept. (They may be able to guess the name based on the term *square root*.)

Solution for #11

A "third of a block" represents a cube root—the number that, when cubed (taken as a factor three times), equals the number you are operating on. You can also show this as an exponent of $\frac{1}{3}$. For example, the cube root of two (written $\sqrt[3]{2}$ or $2^{\frac{1}{3}}$) is approximately equal to 1.259921. You can check that if you take this decimal to the third power, it equals a number very close to 2.

Problem #12

12. Draw a block diagram for the calculation $13^{\frac{1}{2}} \cdot 13^{\frac{1}{3}}$. Use it to write the answer in three forms: (1) a single exponential expression with a base of 13, (2) a single radical, and (3) a decimal approximation.

Questions and Conversations for #12

» *Into how many equal parts should you split each block in order to show powers of both $\frac{1}{2}$ and $\frac{1}{3}$?* Six parts.

Solution for #12

The picture might look like the one shown here. Each small part represents one sixth of a block.

You are joining half of a 13 block to one third of a 13 block. This results in $\frac{5}{6}$ of a 13 block. Some ways to write this are: $13^{\frac{5}{6}}$, $\left(\sqrt[6]{13}\right)^5$, $\sqrt[6]{13^5}$, or approximately 8.4778578.

WRAP UP

Share Strategies

Have students share their strategies and compare results. If they worked on Stage 3 of Exploration 9: Multiplication Slide Rules, you might ask them to compare how the factor blocks and the slide rule representations illustrate the connection between square roots and exponents of $\frac{1}{2}$.

Summarize

Answer any remaining questions that students have. Summarize a few key points:

» You can visualize and analyze meanings and properties of radicals and exponents using a model that represents prime factors as blocks and multiplication as the process of joining the blocks. For example, you can discover connections between exponents and radicals, including the fact that powers of $\frac{1}{2}$ represent square roots: $a^{\frac{1}{2}} = \sqrt{a}$.

» You have discovered some properties of exponents and radicals, including: $\sqrt{a \cdot b} = \sqrt{a} \cdot \sqrt{b}$ (equivalently, $(a \cdot b)^{\frac{1}{2}} = a^{\frac{1}{2}} \cdot b^{\frac{1}{2}}$) and $\left(a^m\right)^n = a^{m \cdot n}$. Because you have explored these properties for a limited number of cases, there may be some numbers for which they are not always true—for example, when a or b is negative.

» You can use definitions and properties of radicals and exponents to name numeric and algebraic expressions in many equivalent ways.

» Expressions containing radicals and fractional exponents can be written in both exact and approximate forms.

Further Exploration

Ask students to think of ways to continue or extend this exploration. Here are some possibilities:

» Continue studying the meanings of expressions that are represented by fractions of blocks. Try performing operations in different orders and investigating the results. When appropriate, use alge-

Teacher's Note. This activity is introductory and exploratory. Students are not necessarily expected to memorize the properties and relationships or to be fully proficient with these calculations. Also, the factor blocks model is a tool for visualization and exploration. It's not meant to provide formal justification for properties of exponents and radicals. On the other hand, it might provide some insight into how you could develop more formal proofs.

braic formulas to express your conjectures. Use your calculator to verify your results as you work.

» What would it look like to simplify expressions involving cube roots? Experiment!

» Create and study your own examples of properties of exponents and radicals. For example, use the factor blocks to explore what happens when you divide numbers that are represented in exponential or radical form. What about when you take roots of roots? Again, consider testing your ideas with a calculator.

Appendix
The Building Blocks Model

Prime numbers are often described as the "building blocks" of the natural numbers. This image suggests that we might actually use blocks to make concrete or pictorial models of prime factorizations. This model is introduced in the "Building Blocks" exploration from the *Factors and Multiples* book in this series.

In this exploration, each prime number between 1 and 50 is assigned a block of its own color. We show multiplication by joining blocks. For example, the prime number 2 is represented by a white block, while the number 3 is shown as red. Because the prime factorization of 6 is $2 \cdot 3$, we "build" the number 6 by joining a white block with a red block.

The students' task is to analyze a page of block diagrams for the numbers 1–50 without being told what they represent, to look for patterns, extend them, and discover the meaning of the blocks. In later activities, they use the Building Blocks model to find relationships between factors and prime factors, explore properties of exponents, and develop new procedures for calculating greatest common factors and least common multiples.

In Exploration 10: "Factor Blocks and Radicals" in this book, we bring this model back, but instead of using colors, we write the prime number on each block. For example the number 6 looks like this:

$$\boxed{2 \mid 3}$$

Because we can reorder and regroup factors however we like without affecting the product, we can do the same with the blocks. For example, we could also show 6 as

$$\boxed{3 \mid 2} \text{ or } \boxed{\begin{array}{c} 3 \\ 2 \end{array}}$$

To prepare students for Exploration 10, ask them to find prime factorizations and draw block diagrams for a set of numbers such as 36, 84, 90, 96, and 98. The answers are:

36	84	90	96	98
$\boxed{2\mid2\mid3\mid3}$	$\boxed{2\mid2\mid3\mid7}$	$\boxed{2\mid3\mid3\mid5}$	$\boxed{2\mid2\mid2\mid2\mid2\mid3}$	$\boxed{2\mid7\mid7}$

These drawings show the blocks arranged in horizontal strings with the prime factors in order. This is often a convenient way to do it, but again, students may arrange the blocks as they like.

Next, ask the students to write the prime factorizations for these numbers in exponential form. They should get

$$36 = 2^2 \cdot 3^2, \; 84 = 2^2 \cdot 3^1 \cdot 7^1, \; 90 = 2^1 \cdot 3^2 \cdot 5^1, \; 96 = 2^5 \cdot 3^1, \text{ and } 98 = 2^1 \cdot 7^2.$$

Finally, ask them how the exponents relate to the block diagrams. They will probably have little trouble seeing that the exponent counts the number of blocks for each prime factor. This is a key idea in the "Factor Blocks and Radicals" exploration.

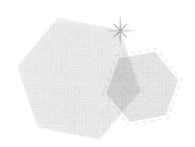

References

Bell, M., Bretzlauf, J., Dillard, A., Hartfield, R., Isaccs, A., McBride, J., . . . Saecker, P. (2007). *Everyday mathematics: Teacher's lesson guide, grade 5 volume 1* (3rd ed.). Chicago, IL: McGraw Hill.

National Governors Association Center for Best Practices, & Council of Chief State School Officers. (2010). Common core state standards for mathematics. Washington, DC: Authors.

Sheffield, L. J. (2003). *Extending the challenge in mathematics: Developing mathematical promise in K–8 students.* Thousand Oaks, CA: Corwin Press

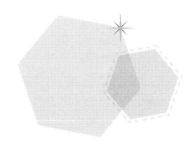

About the Author

Jerry Burkhart has been teaching and learning math with gifted students in Minnesota for nearly 20 years. He has degrees in physics, mathematics, and math education. He provides professional development for teachers and is a regular presenter at conferences around topics of meeting the needs of gifted students in mathematics.

Common Core State Standards Alignment

Exploration	Common Core State Standards in Mathematics
Exploration 1: Triangle Sums	5.NBT.B Perform operations with multi-digit whole numbers and with decimals to hundredths. 5.OA.A Write and interpret numerical expressions. 5.OA.B Analyze patterns and relationships.
Exploration 2: Torran Math	5.NBT.A Understand the place value system. 5.OA.B Analyze patterns and relationships.
Exploration 3: Number Line Magnifiers	5.NBT.A Understand the place value system. 5.NBT.B Perform operations with multi-digit whole numbers and with decimals to hundredths.
Exploration 4: Million, Billion, Trillion . . .	5.NBT.A Understand the place value system. 8.EE.A Work with radicals and integer exponents. 5.MD.A Convert like measurement units within a given measurement system.
Exploration 5: Discovering Divisibility Tests	5.NBT.A Understand the place value system. 4.OA.B Gain familiarity with factors and multiples. 6.EE.A Apply and extend previous understandings of arithmetic to algebraic expressions.
Exploration 6: Visualizing Decimal Multiplication	5.NBT.B Perform operations with multi-digit whole numbers and with decimals to hundredths. 6.NS.B Compute fluently with multi-digit numbers and find common factors and multiples. 6.EE.A Apply and extend previous understandings of arithmetic to algebraic expressions.
Exploration 7: Think Like a Torran!	5.NBT.A Understand the place value system. 5.NBT.B Perform operations with multi-digit whole numbers and with decimals to hundredths.
Exploration 8: Extreme Calculations	5.NBT.A Understand the place value system. 8.EE.A Work with radicals and integer exponents. 5.MD.A Convert like measurement units within a given measurement system.
Exploration 9: Multiplication Slide Rules	6.NS.C Apply and extend previous understandings of numbers to the system of rational numbers. 8.EE.A Work with radicals and integer exponents. 5.NBT.A Understand the place value system.

Exploration	Common Core State Standards in Mathematics
Exploration 9: Multiplication Slide Rules, *continued*	7.NS.A Apply and extend previous understandings of operations with fractions. 8.NS.A Know that there are numbers that are not rational, and approximate them by rational numbers.
Exploration 10: Factor Blocks and Radicals	7.EE.A Use properties of operations to generate equivalent expressions. 8.EE.A Work with radicals and integer exponents. 6.NS.B Compute fluently with multi-digit numbers and find common factors and multiples. 6.EE.A Apply and extend previous understandings of arithmetic to algebraic expressions.

Note: Please see p. 8 of the book for details on how to connect and extend the core learning of content in these lessons.